Simon & Schuster
Children's Guide to Sea Creatures

Ram's horn shell encrusted with barnacles

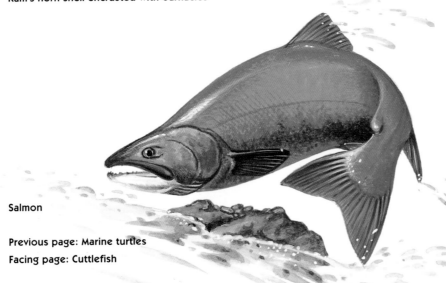

Salmon

Previous page: Marine turtles
Facing page: Cuttlefish

Simon & Schuster
Children's Guide to Sea Creatures

JINNY JOHNSON

Simon & Schuster Books for Young Readers

SIMON & SCHUSTER BOOKS FOR YOUNG READERS
An imprint of Simon & Schuster Children's Publishing Division
1230 Avenue of the Americas, New York, New York 10020

Copyright © 1998 by Marshall Editions
All rights reserved including the right of reproduction in whole
or in part in any form.

SIMON & SCHUSTER BOOKS FOR YOUNG READERS
is a trademark of Simon & Schuster.

This book was conceived, edited, and designed by Marshall Editions
The Old Brewery, 6 Blundell Street, London N7 9BH, UK

First American Edition, 1998
Originated in Singapore by Master Image
Printed and bound in China by
Toppan Leefung Printed Limited
0413 TOP
20 19 18 17 16 15 14 13 12 11

Library of Congress Cataloging-in-Publication Data
Johnson, Jinny
Simon & Schuster children's guide to marine animals/Jinny Johnson.
p.   cm.
Summary: Describes the major groups of marine animals, including fish,
birds, mammals, and crustaceans.
ISBN-13: 978-0-689-81534-8 (ISBN-10: 0-689-81534-4)
1. Marine animals— Juvenile literature. [1. Marine animals.]
I. Title
QL122.2.J64 1998
591.77— dc21
97-8227
CIP
AC

The publisher gratefully acknowledges
Dr. Gregory Hinkle's expert help and
advice, and thanks him for his
contribution to this project.

Consultant: **Professor Philip Whitfield**
Managing Editor: **Kate Phelps**
Art Editor: **Dave Goodman**
Picture Editor: **Zilda Tandy**
Copy Editor: **Jolika Feszt**

Editorial Director: **Cynthia O'Brien**
Art Director: **Ralph Pitchford**
Production: **Janice Storr, Selby Sinton**

Contents

Cormorant

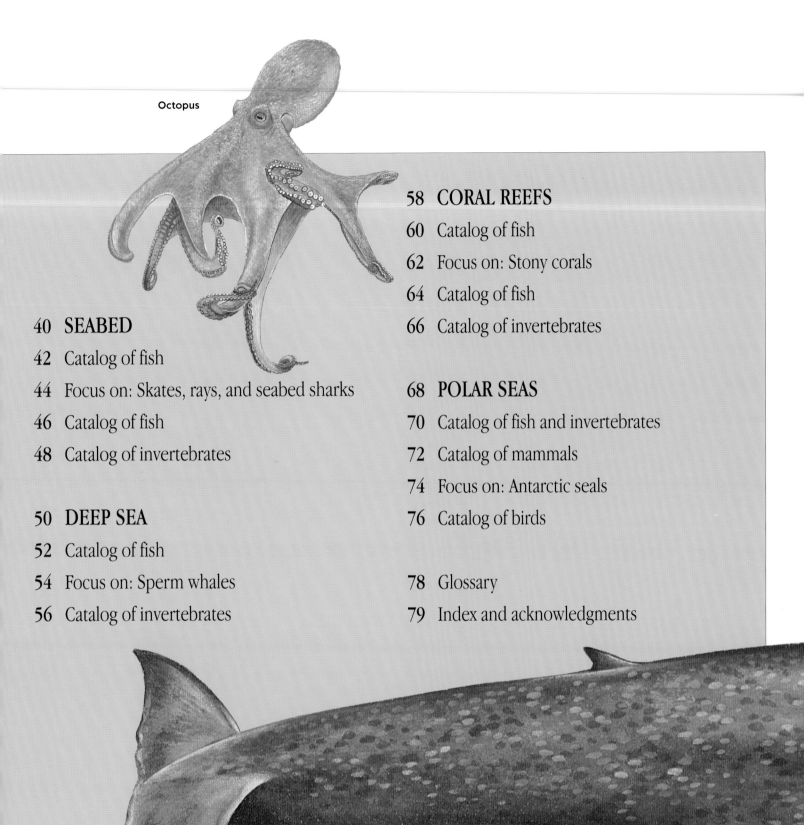

Octopus

Blue whale

Foreword

When you watch waves breaking on a beach or look out over the ocean from the deck of a boat, it's hard to imagine all of the life that exists under the water's surface. But life has thrived in the ocean for over four billion years—far longer than on land. Animals that spend their lives under and around the water have adapted in an astonishing variety of ways to survive life in the ocean.

Living creatures need oxygen. But the molecules of oxygen in the oceans are dissolved in water. Fish, sharks, and many other marine animals can extract dissolved oxygen from water as it flows past their gills. Mammals like whales and seals don't have gills, so they have to return to the surface to breathe. But they don't need to breathe nearly as often as people do. Sperm whales can stay underwater without breathing for 45 minutes at a time.

Animals that live on the seashore, where the water meets the land, have to survive crashing waves and changing tides, which can cover them with water or leave them exposed to the air. Some creatures, like barnacles and mussels, cling tightly to rocks

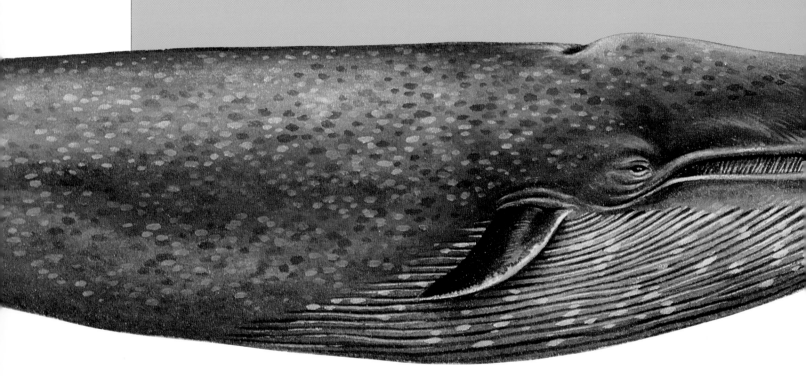

Blue whale

to avoid being swept away by waves. Clams bury themselves deep in the sand; crabs find shelter among rocks.

No sunlight penetrates the deepest parts of the ocean. Below 3,300 feet the water is completely dark and no plants can grow. But there is life here too. Fish and other creatures hunt each other and scavenge food that drifts down from the sunlit waters above. Some fish even have chemicals in their bodies that make them glow in the dark, attracting prey.

The seas around the north and south poles are so cold that salt water freezes. How do the animals which live there survive? Whales and seals have a thick layer of fat, called blubber, under their skins, which acts like a warm coat and keeps them from freezing. A fish called the Antarctic cod has a special type of "antifreeze" in its body that keeps its blood from turning to ice.

From warm tropical waters to icy polar seas, from colorful coral reefs to the lightless depths, oceans cover two thirds of the earth's surface. More of the land on this planet is underwater than is above. Human beings have studied and mapped every continent, but much of the land under the sea is still unknown to us. The ocean is a fascinating and mysterious world, waiting to be explored.

PROFESSOR PHILIP WHITFIELD

Dolphin

The world of the sea

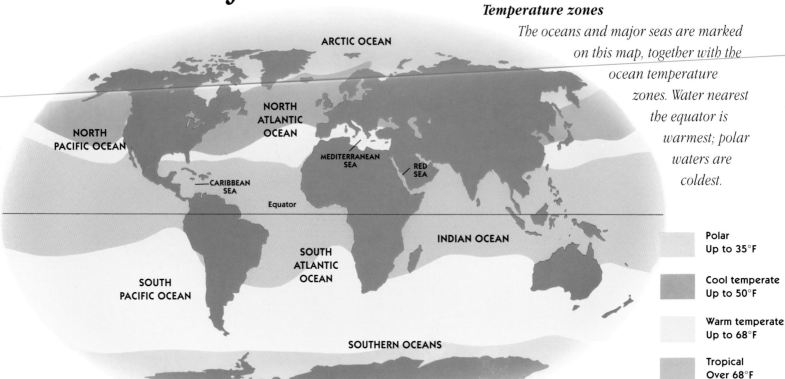

Temperature zones

The oceans and major seas are marked on this map, together with the ocean temperature zones. Water nearest the equator is warmest; polar waters are coldest.

ARCTIC OCEAN

NORTH ATLANTIC OCEAN

NORTH PACIFIC OCEAN

MEDITERRANEAN SEA

RED SEA

CARIBBEAN SEA

Equator

INDIAN OCEAN

SOUTH ATLANTIC OCEAN

SOUTH PACIFIC OCEAN

SOUTHERN OCEANS

Polar
Up to 35°F

Cool temperate
Up to 50°F

Warm temperate
Up to 68°F

Tropical
Over 68°F

Earth is often known as the watery planet because oceans cover two thirds of its surface. About 97 percent of the world's water is in the oceans. There are no borders and all the waters flow into one another, but the different areas are given separate names. Large expanses, such as the Atlantic and Pacific, are called oceans; smaller areas, such as the Caribbean and Mediterranean, are seas.

Everyone knows that the water in the sea is salty. These salts come from the land. As fresh water runs over rocks and along rivers, it picks up mineral salts from the soil. Eventually these salts are carried by rivers into the sea. Over billions of years, enough salt has been washed into the ocean to make the water taste salty.

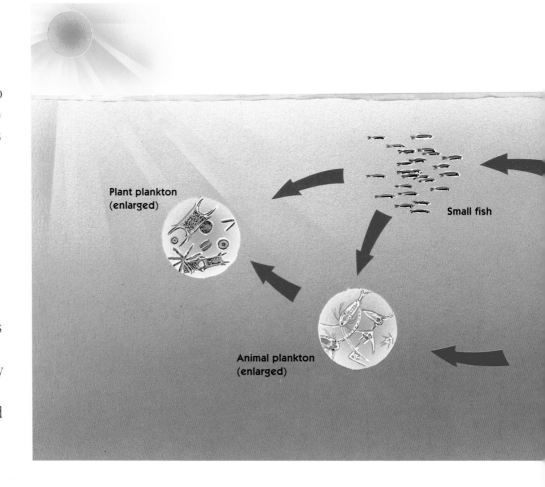

Plant plankton (enlarged)

Small fish

Animal plankton (enlarged)

A typical fish

A fish moves by wavelike movements of its body. The fins help it change direction, slow down, or move up or down in the water.

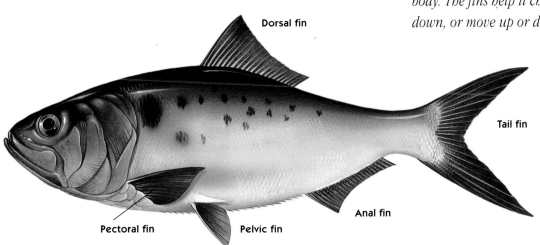

Dorsal fin

Tail fin

Anal fin

Pectoral fin

Pelvic fin

Life manages to survive in all parts of the ocean, but the most highly populated waters are those near the surface. Here plenty of light penetrates to about 330 feet and plant plankton thrive. These microscopic plants are eaten by animal plankton—tiny animals that drift in surface waters. Animal plankton includes two types of creatures—those which remain plankton all their lives and those which only drift with the plankton while they are larvae. Eventually they develop into adult animals, such as crabs and barnacles, with different lifestyles.

Among the larger creatures in the oceans there are at least 160,000 species of invertebrates—animals without backbones—creatures such as clams, mussels, and crabs (see page 11). They live in every part of the ocean from the surface waters to the deepest sea. Of the vertebrates—animals with backbones—fish are the most common. There are at least 14,000 different kinds of fish, ranging from tiny gobies, which are less than an

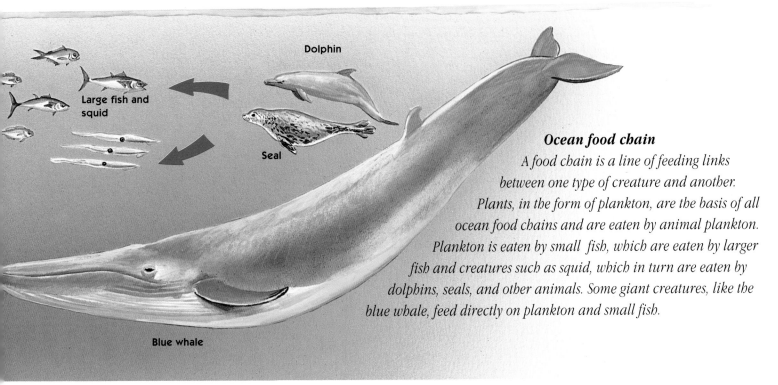

Dolphin

Large fish and squid

Seal

Blue whale

Ocean food chain

A food chain is a line of feeding links between one type of creature and another. Plants, in the form of plankton, are the basis of all ocean food chains and are eaten by animal plankton. Plankton is eaten by small fish, which are eaten by larger fish and creatures such as squid, which in turn are eaten by dolphins, seals, and other animals. Some giant creatures, like the blue whale, feed directly on plankton and small fish.

PLANKTON

A bucket of seawater may look clear and lifeless, but in fact it contains thousands of tiny life forms called plankton. There are two kinds of plankton—plant plankton and animal plankton. Plant plankton (below) are so small that they cannot be seen without a microscope. They use the sun's energy to make new living material. Animal plankton (right) are tiny creatures that feed on plant plankton and on each other. The biggest are about half an inch long.

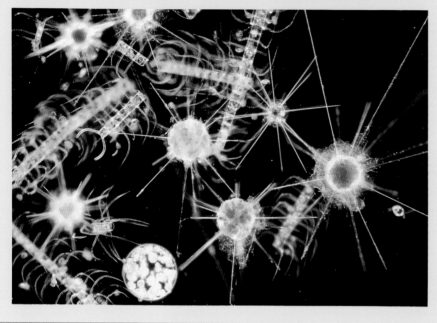

inch long, to the whale shark, which grows 40 to 60 feet long. There are a few marine reptiles, including sea snakes, marine turtles, and one lizard—the marine iguana. Many types of birds, such as gannets, gulls, and petrels depend on the sea for their food and nest on shores and sea cliffs. Other birds, such as penguins, are expert swimmers.

Finally there are a number of mammals, such as whales and seals, that have adapted to life in the sea. The 78 species of whales, including the blue whale, live their whole lives in the sea and cannot survive out of it. Seals and sea lions have not adapted as fully to marine life. They spend much of their lives in the sea, but they still come to land to breed and to give birth.

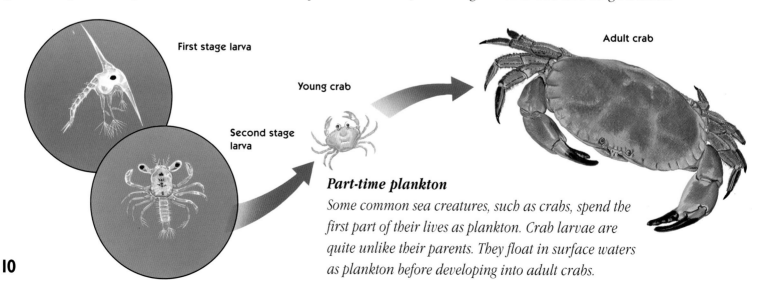

First stage larva

Young crab

Second stage larva

Adult crab

Part-time plankton

Some common sea creatures, such as crabs, spend the first part of their lives as plankton. Crab larvae are quite unlike their parents. They float in surface waters as plankton before developing into adult crabs.

INVERTEBRATE ANIMALS

There are many more invertebrates—animals without backbones—in the sea than any other type of animal, but we know much less about them than we do about sharks, whales, and seals. Here are six of the most common groups of marine invertebrates, more examples of which you will find on the following pages.

SPONGES

Sponges are the simplest many-celled animals. Their shapes vary from tiny cups, tubelike pipes, and tall vases, to rounded masses. Special filtering cells in their bodies trap food particles in the water.

Vase sponge

Glass sponge

CNIDARIANS

The Cnidaria group includes creatures such as jellyfish, sea anemones, and corals. Most have tubelike bodies with a central mouth surrounded by tentacles. There are stinging cells on the tentacles.

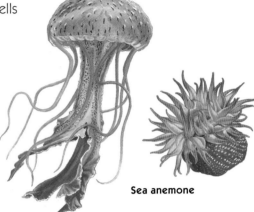

Jellyfish

Sea anemone

SEGMENTED WORMS

There are almost 6,000 species of sea-living segmented worms, divided into two groups. The first, containing species such as paddle worms, move about to find food. The second, including species such as feather duster worms, spend their lives in a tube or burrow and filter food from the water.

Paddle worm

Feather duster worm

MOLLUSKS

There are at least 100,000 living species of mollusks. The three main groups are the gastropods—creatures such as limpets; the bivalves—clams, mussels, and scallops; and cephalopods—squid, cuttlefish and octopus.

Clam

Squid

ECHINODERMS

There are four main groups of echinoderms—brittle stars, starfish, sea cucumbers, and sea urchins and sand dollars. Many have a body that is divided into five parts with a mouth at one end and anus at the other. Most echinoderms move around using tiny stilts called tube feet, each tipped with a sucking disk.

Starfish

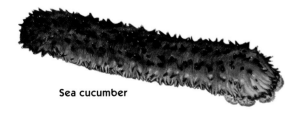

Sea cucumber

CRUSTACEANS

There are about 31,000 species of crustaceans, including creatures such as barnacles, crabs, lobsters, and shrimps. Most have a tough outer skeleton, a number of walking and mouthpart appendages, and two pairs of antennae.

Barnacle

Shrimp

11

Seashore

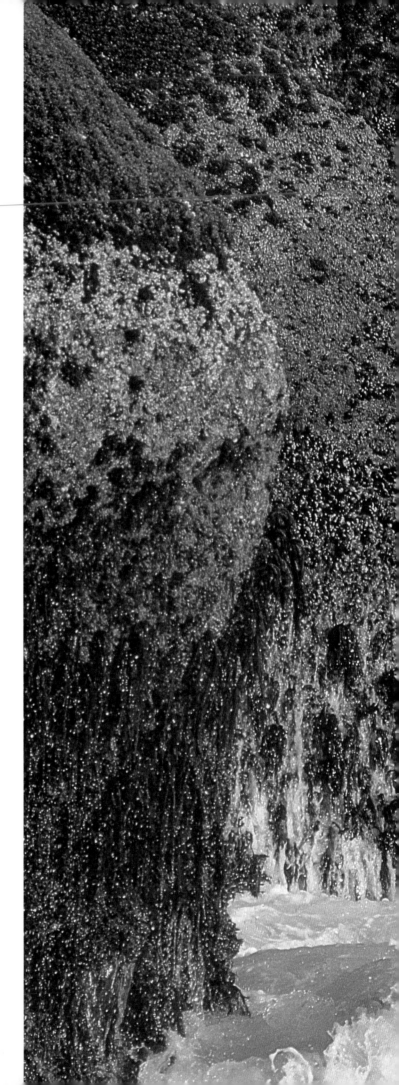

The meeting place of land and sea, where a wide variety of creatures have found ways of surviving the changing tides.

Land and ocean meet at the seashore, where waves crash over rocks or creep up sandy beaches. A huge range of fish and invertebrates live in the waters fringing the shore, while others are adapted to live on the shore itself. Because tides come in and out twice a day, these creatures have difficult lives—some of the day they are plunged underwater; at other times they are left exposed to the sun, wind, or cold night air. Many inhabitants of the seashore, such as limpets and winkles, protect their soft bodies with hard shells. Others shelter in burrows or under rocks.

Animals and plants on a rocky shore have to find ways of hanging on when waves break over them. Seaweeds have tough, rootlike bases called holdfasts. Mussels tie themselves down with a "beard" of strong threads. Starfish and sea urchins cling with hundreds of tiny tubular feet, each tipped with a suction disk. Crabs and shrimps do not hang onto rocks but remain hidden under ledges in rock pools when the tide goes out.

A sandy or muddy shore may look empty of life, but here, too, there is a huge variety of animals, including worms, clams, and crabs, many of them hidden in burrows underground. Tiny holes or trails in the sand may be the only signs of their presence.

The seashore, with its waves and tides, is a turbulent habitat for marine animals and plants.

Paddle worm

This worm lives under rocks among seaweed, both on the shore and in deeper water. It has four pairs of tentacles on its head and lots of tiny leaflike paddles down each side of its long body. It feeds on other worms.

FOUND IN:
Atlantic and Pacific coasts

SIZE:
Up to 18 in long

SCIENTIFIC NAME:
***Phyllodoce* spp.**

Sea anemone

The sea anemone may look like a flower, but it is actually an animal that catches other creatures to eat. At one end of its body is a sucking disk that keeps it attached to a rock. At the other end is the mouth, surrounded by tentacles.

FOUND IN:
Atlantic and Pacific coasts

SIZE:
Up to 10 in tall

SCIENTIFIC NAME:
***Tealia* spp.**

Sea mouse

Despite its plump shape, the sea mouse is actually a kind of worm. Its upper side is covered with lots of grayish-brown hairs which give it a furry look and inspire its common name. The sea mouse spends much of its life under mud or sand in shallow water.

FOUND IN:
Atlantic and Mediterranean coasts

SIZE:
7 in long

SCIENTIFIC NAME:
Aphrodita aculeata

Oyster

FOUND IN:
Atlantic and Pacific coasts

SIZE:
Up to 4 in long

SCIENTIFIC NAME:
***Ostrea* spp.**

The oyster is a type of mollusk. It has a soft body protected by two hard shells, which are held together by strong muscles. It eats tiny pieces of plant and animal food, which it filters from the water. The water is drawn into the partly opened shell and any food is caught on tiny sticky hairs on the gills.

Chromodoris nudibranch

Nudibranches, or sea slugs, are related to snails, but they have no shells and are often brightly colored. This species has a pair of hornlike projections and a clump of feathery gills on its back. Sponges are its main food.

FOUND IN:
Pacific coasts

SIZE:
6 in long

SCIENTIFIC NAME:
Chromodoris elisabethina

Cuttlefish

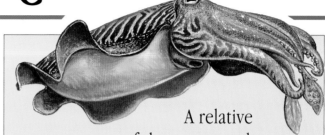

A relative of the octopus, the cuttlefish has eight arms and two long tentacles. It uses all of these to catch crabs and other prey. Inside the body is a spongy shell. These shells sometimes wash up on the shore.

FOUND IN:
Atlantic and Mediterranean coasts

SIZE:
Up to 15 in long

SCIENTIFIC NAME:
Sepia officinalis

Octopus

The octopus has a pouchlike body and eight long arms lined with two rows of suckers. It pulls itself along with its strong arms and can also swim quickly by shooting jets of water out of its body. It spends much of its time hiding in crevices or under rocks, watching out for prey such as crabs, clams, and shrimps. The octopus holds its prey in its tentacles and may kill or paralyze it with a poisonous bite.

FOUND IN:
Atlantic coasts

SIZE:
Up to 40 in long

SCIENTIFIC NAME:
Octopus vulgaris

FOCUS ON: *Rock clingers*

While most marine creatures swim or float freely in the water, some live firmly attached to rocks or other surfaces. This helps protect them from the waves that sweep over them twice a day as the tide comes in. Barnacles, one kind of rock clinger, are among the most common creatures on the shore. Huge colonies of them cover rocks and shore debris, and even attach themselves to other creatures such as mussels. Barnacles begin life as free-swimming larvae and spend a month or more floating in coastal waters, feeding on plankton. During its final larval stage, each barnacle finds somewhere to settle. It fixes itself to the surface with a cementlike substance that it makes in glands in its body. Once settled, it does not move again. Limpets, periwinkles, and chitons can all cling to rocks by means of a suckerlike foot, which is so strong that they are almost impossible to move. But all these creatures can also move around on their own to graze on algae.

Common mussel

The threads that hold the mussel onto rocks are made as a sticky fluid inside a gland in the mussel's body. This fluid hardens to keep the mussel firmly in place. The mussel's shell is in two halves. These are normally held tight together, but they can be partly opened so that the mussel can filter tiny pieces of food from the water.

Rough periwinkle

There are many different types of periwinkle, each adapted for life in different parts of the shore. The rough periwinkle lives on stones and rocks higher up the shore than most other species.

Common limpet

As limpets move over rocks feeding on algae, they leave a sticky trail of mucus behind them. This helps each limpet make its way back to the exact same place on the rock after each feeding trip.

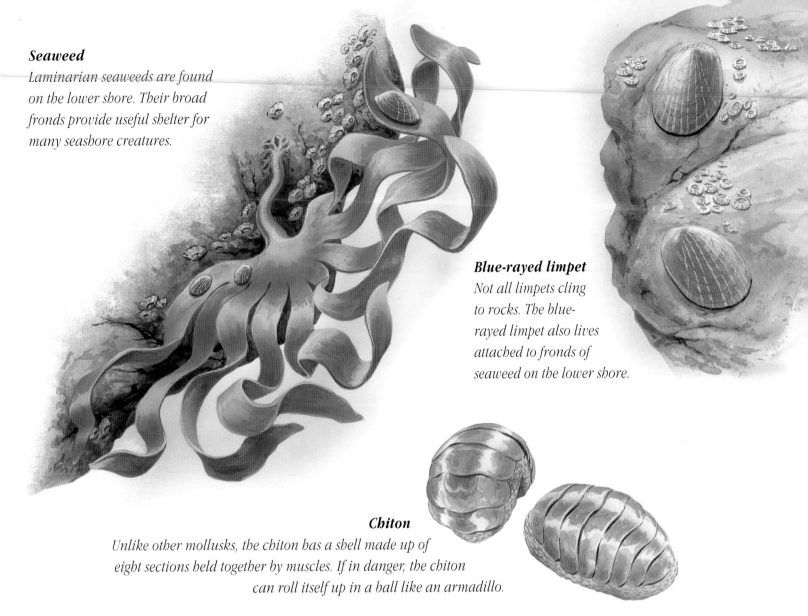

Seaweed

Laminarian seaweeds are found on the lower shore. Their broad fronds provide useful shelter for many seashore creatures.

Blue-rayed limpet

Not all limpets cling to rocks. The blue-rayed limpet also lives attached to fronds of seaweed on the lower shore.

Chiton

Unlike other mollusks, the chiton has a shell made up of eight sections held together by muscles. If in danger, the chiton can roll itself up in a ball like an armadillo.

Acorn barnacle

When covered by water at high tide, the barnacle opens its shell at the top and puts out its feathery arms to gather plankton to eat. When the tide is out, the barnacle keeps its trapdoor top firmly closed.

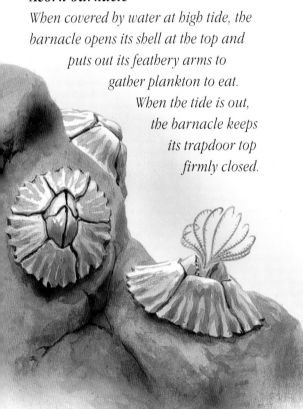

Feeding barnacle

A giant acorn barnacle with its plates open for feeding. These barnacles can grow up to 3½ inches tall.

Hermit crab

Unlike other crabs, the hermit crab has no hard shell of its own. It protects its soft body by living in the discarded shell of another creature, such as a snail. The crab has large pincers on its first pair of legs which it uses to grab its prey.

FOUND IN:
**North
Atlantic coasts**

SIZE:
Up to 4 in long

SCIENTIFIC NAME:
Pagurus bernhardus

Razor clam

The razor clam is a type of mollusk, with a long, narrow shell. It lives in burrows in sandy shores and can bury itself extremely quickly if threatened. It feeds on tiny plants and animals, which it filters from the water.

FOUND IN:
**Atlantic and
Pacific coasts**

SIZE:
Up to 8 in long

SCIENTIFIC NAME:
Ensis siliqua

Common sand dollar

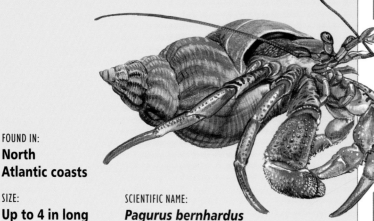

The sand dollar has a flattened disklike body and a shell covered with short spines. On its underside are rows of tubelike feet, which help it gather tiny pieces of food.

FOUND IN:
**North Atlantic and
Pacific coasts**

SIZE:
3 in across

SCIENTIFIC NAME:
*Echinarachnius
parma*

Edible crab

Most crabs have a strong shell, which protects the body, and five pairs of legs. On the first pair of these are powerful pincers used to break open the shells of prey, such as mollusks. The other legs are smaller. Crabs live among rocks on the lower shore.

Amphipod

This small crustacean lives on the lower shore under rocks or among seaweed, and feeds on tiny pieces of plant and animal matter. On its abdomen are three pairs of swimming legs and three pairs of jumping legs.

FOUND IN:
Atlantic and Pacific coasts

SIZE:
Up to 1 in long

SCIENTIFIC NAME:
Gammarus locusta

Lobster

FOUND IN:
North Atlantic coasts

SIZE:
12 in

SCIENTIFIC NAME:
Homarus americanus

During the day this large crustacean hides in rock crevices, but at night it comes out to hunt. It uses its huge pincers to crack and tear apart prey such as mollusks and crabs.

Montague's shrimp

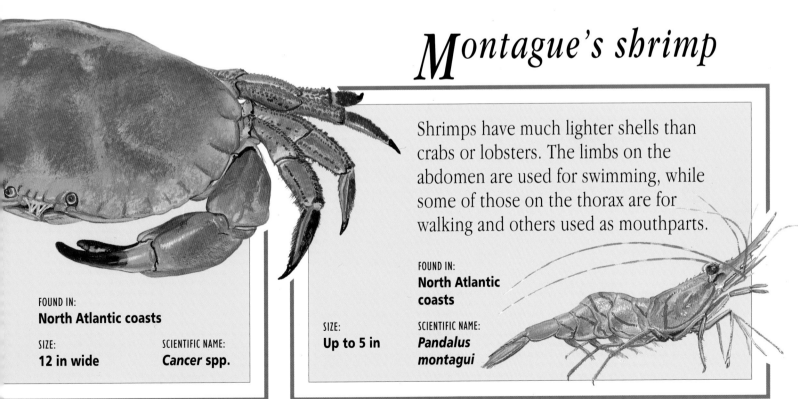

Shrimps have much lighter shells than crabs or lobsters. The limbs on the abdomen are used for swimming, while some of those on the thorax are for walking and others used as mouthparts.

FOUND IN:
North Atlantic coasts

SIZE:
Up to 5 in

SCIENTIFIC NAME:
Pandalus montagui

FOUND IN:
North Atlantic coasts

SIZE:
12 in wide

SCIENTIFIC NAME:
Cancer spp.

FOCUS ON: *Coastal birds*

Coastal birds, such as gulls, gannets, and cormorants, do not spend much time actually in the water, but they do depend on the sea for food. All are hunters, feeding mostly on fish and squid, and each type of bird has its own fishing technique.

Gannets, for example, are superb divers. Having sighted prey from as high as 100 feet above the surface, the gannet plunges down with its neck and beak held straight out and its wings swept back to make its body as streamlined as possible. Cormorants make gentler dives from the surface. Once underwater, they push themselves along with their strong webbed feet and snap up prey with their hooked beaks. Guillemots also pursue prey under the surface, flapping their wings as though flying through the water.

Gulls are the scavengers of the shore. They do hunt fish, but they also eat up waste from fishing boats and take food from garbage dumps.

Gannet
Several special features help make the gannet an expert diver. Its nostril openings are covered with bony flaps so that water cannot get into them when the bird dives. Salt glands above the eyes help get rid of the salt the bird takes in from seawater and fish. And air-filled spaces in the head take some of the impact of the high-speed dive.

Oystercatchers
Adult oystercatchers are expert at opening mollusk and crab shells with their bright red beaks. Young birds stay with their parents for up to a year learning feeding techniques.

Guillemot

Black-headed gull

Guillemot and black-headed gull
Like most seabirds, guillemots have webbed feet which help them swim well but make movement more difficult on land. Both these birds nest in huge colonies on cliff tops or rocks. Black-headed gulls rarely dive for fish but they do sometimes steal food from other seabirds.

Cliff nest
A black-legged kittiwake and her chick cling to their nest on a narrow cliff ledge. There they are safely out of the reach of most predators.

Brown pelican
This pelican dives from as high as 30 feet above the water. As it enters the water it opens its beak and traps its prey in its pouch. Sometimes brown pelicans fly together in large flocks and plunge-dive together.

Cormorant
The cormorant catches fish and other prey during dives lasting up to half a minute. It usually returns to the surface and shakes the water off its food before eating. After feeding the cormorant often rests on rocks or cliffs with its wings spread out to dry.

Bluehead wrasse

This is one of several hundred species of wrasse, found all over the world in tropical and warm waters. Most are brightly colored and feed on crustaceans, particularly crabs, which they crush with their strong teeth. Only male bluehead wrasse have the bright blue coloring that gives this species its name. Small males and all females are mostly yellow in color.

FOUND IN:
Warm Atlantic waters and Caribbean Sea

SIZE:
6 in long

SCIENTIFIC NAME:
Thalassoma bifasciatum

Seahorse

The seahorse, with its curling tail and horselike head, looks unlike any other fish. It moves slowly, gently pushing itself along with movements of the small fin on its back, and it can attach itself to seaweed by means of its tail. Another unusual feature of the seahorse is that the male has a pouch on his body where the female lays her eggs to be incubated.

FOUND IN:
West Atlantic Ocean and Caribbean Sea

SIZE:
1½ in long

SCIENTIFIC NAME:
Hippocampus zosterae

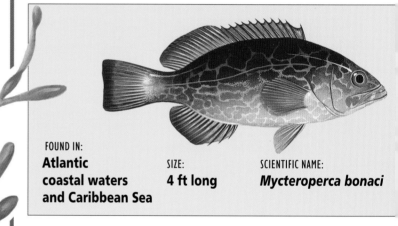

FOUND IN:
Atlantic coastal waters and Caribbean Sea

SIZE:
4 ft long

SCIENTIFIC NAME:
Mycteroperca bonaci

Blackeye goby

FOUND IN:
Pacific coastal waters

SIZE:
6 in long

SCIENTIFIC NAME:
Coryphopterus nicholsi

Moray

Black grouper

FOUND IN:
Atlantic coastal waters and Mediterranean Sea

SIZE:
4½ ft long

SCIENTIFIC NAME:
Muraena helana

The grouper is not a particularly fast-moving fish and tends to lurk among rocks, waiting for prey to swim by. When a fish comes near, the grouper opens its large mouth and sucks in the prey with a mouthful of water.

Like all of the 100 or so different species of moray found in warm seas, this moray has a scaleless, boldly patterned body, powerful jaws, and strong, sharp teeth. During the day it hides among rocks, but at night it is a fierce hunter, catching prey such as other fish and squid.

Gunnel

Most gobies have a blunt head and a long, slender body. The two pelvic fins are joined together forming a sucking disk on the belly, which the fish uses to attach itself to rocks or other surfaces.

The gunnel, or butterfish, has a flattened eel-like body. It is common around rocky shores, where it feeds on shrimps and mollusks.

FOUND IN:
North Atlantic coastal waters

SIZE:
8 in long

SCIENTIFIC NAME:
Pholis gunnellus

Marine iguana

The marine iguana is the only lizard that spends most of its life in the sea, swimming and diving as it searches for seaweed, its main food. When in the water, the iguana uses its powerful tail to push itself along. It has to come to the surface to breathe, but when it dives, its heart rate slows while the body uses less oxygen.

FOUND IN:
**Pacific Ocean:
coasts of Galapagos Islands**

SIZE:
4–5 ft long

SCIENTIFIC NAME:
Amblyrhynchus cristatus

American manatee

The manatee is a plant-eating marine mammal, with flipperlike front limbs. There are three nails on each flipper which are used for gathering food. The manatee spends much of its time on the seabed, but it has to come to the surface to breathe.

FOUND IN:
**Atlantic coast of Florida and
Gulf of Mexico**

SIZE:
Up to 10 ft long

SCIENTIFIC NAME:
Trichechus manatus

California sea lion

Sea lions feed on fish and squid and spend most of their lives at sea. But they mate and give birth on land. Unlike seals, they can bend their hind flippers forward so that they can move more easily on land.

FOUND IN:
**Pacific coast of
North America**

SIZE:
Up to 8 ft long

SCIENTIFIC NAME:
Zalophus californianus

Caspian tern

FOUND IN:
**Coasts worldwide,
except South America**

SIZE:
Body: 19–23 in long

SCIENTIFIC NAME:
Sterna caspia

The Caspian is the largest of the terns and has a bright orange, daggerlike beak. It feeds on fish and dives into the sea to catch its prey. Although this species of tern is very widespread, it breeds only on quiet, remote coasts or marshlands near rich feeding areas. It lays its two or three eggs in a hollow scraped in the ground.

Great black-backed gull

One of the largest gulls, this bird is a fierce predator. It hunts other seabirds, such as puffins and petrels, and takes their eggs and young as well as fish. It also scavenges on garbage around fishing ports and on the shore.

FOUND IN:
**Atlantic coasts
of North America and Europe**

SIZE:
Body: 28–31 in long

SCIENTIFIC NAME:
Larus marinus

Sea otter

The sea otter spends nearly all of its life at sea, often among huge beds of kelp seaweed. It feeds on clams, sea urchins, and other creatures which it eats while lying in the water. It often uses a rock to break the shells of its prey. At night, the sea otter wraps itself in fronds of kelp so it does not drift out to sea while asleep.

FOUND IN:
Pacific coast of North America

SIZE:
Body up to 3 ft long; tail up to 13 in

SCIENTIFIC NAME:
Enhydra lutris

Open ocean

There are few hiding places in the waters of the open ocean, so its inhabitants must find other ways of keeping safe.

The vast areas of open ocean far from land are little known to most of us. But beneath the surface, a range of creatures from jellyfish to whales cruise the seemingly endless waters.

Life is less abundant in the open ocean than in waters nearer land. Shallow coastal seas are rich in nutrients washed down from the land and this encourages the growth of plankton, the minute plants and animals that live in the water. In the open ocean there are fewer nutrients and therefore less plankton, the basis of all ocean life. An advantage, though, of the open sea is that it is less subject to dramatic change than the coast, which is covered and uncovered by tides twice each day.

One particular problem for the creatures living in the open sea is that, unlike those in coastal waters and the shore, they have nowhere to hide so they need other ways of protecting themselves. Some, such as jellyfish and the Portuguese man-of-war, have stinging cells on their tentacles, which help them to defend themselves against enemies as well as to catch prey. Many small fish, such as herring, sardines, and anchovies, gather in huge schools and find safety in numbers. Larger fish, such as tuna and marlin, have few enemies. They are high speed swimmers, able to travel huge distances to find their prey.

A pair of bottlenose dolphins make graceful leaps out of the water, rising as high as 15 feet above the surface.

Swordfish

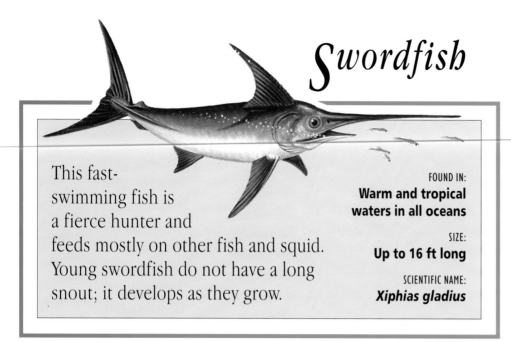

This fast-swimming fish is a fierce hunter and feeds mostly on other fish and squid. Young swordfish do not have a long snout; it develops as they grow.

FOUND IN:
Warm and tropical waters in all oceans

SIZE:
Up to 16 ft long

SCIENTIFIC NAME:
Xiphias gladius

Blue marlin

FOUND IN:
Warm and tropical waters in all oceans

SIZE:
Up to 15 ft long

SCIENTIFIC NAME:
Makaira nigricans

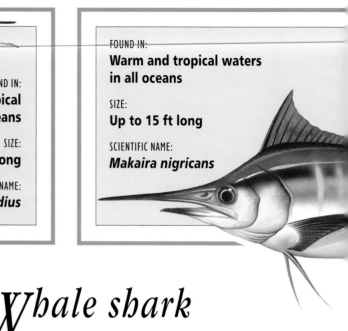

Hammerhead shark

The hammerhead has a broad head that extends to each side. There is one eye and one nostril on either side of the elongated head. This spacing of eyes and nostrils may improve the shark's sight and sense of smell.

FOUND IN:
All oceans

SIZE:
14 ft long

SCIENTIFIC NAME:
Sphyrna zygaena

Whale shark

The whale shark is the biggest fish in the world. Despite its huge size, it is not a fierce hunter and feeds on plankton and small fish, which it filters from the water. The shark opens its huge mouth and takes in a rush of water containing lots of small creatures. The water flows out again through the gill slits, leaving the food in the mouth. The whale shark often follows and eats fish swimming together in a school.

*M*anta ray

The blue marlin is one of the fastest of all fish and has the crescent-shaped tail typical of high-speed swimmers.

With its huge, pointed fins, the manta is the biggest ray. Like the whale shark, this giant feeds mostly on plankton, which it filters from the water. It also eats fish. The manta often basks near the surface with the tips of its fins out of the water.

FOUND IN:
Warm and tropical waters in all oceans

SIZE:
Up to 22 ft long

SCIENTIFIC NAME:
Manta birostris

FOUND IN:
All oceans

SIZE:
Usually 40 ft long but may be up to 60 ft

SCIENTIFIC NAME:
Rhincodon typus

*F*lying fish

The flying fish has a dramatic way of escaping its enemies—it leaps up and glides over the surface of the water with the aid of its large, winglike fins. It can glide as far as 300 feet, up to 5 feet above the surface.

FOUND IN:
North Atlantic Ocean

SIZE:
Up to 17 in long

SCIENTIFIC NAME:
Cypselurus melanurus

Herring

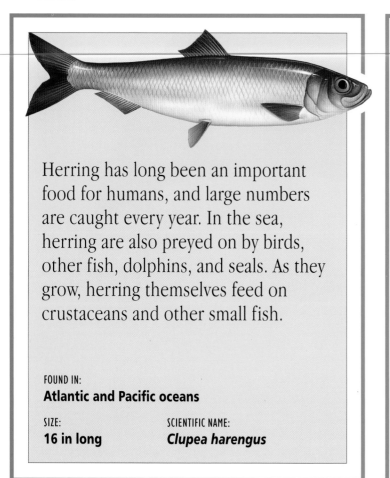

Herring has long been an important food for humans, and large numbers are caught every year. In the sea, herring are also preyed on by birds, other fish, dolphins, and seals. As they grow, herring themselves feed on crustaceans and other small fish.

FOUND IN:
Atlantic and Pacific oceans

SIZE:
16 in long

SCIENTIFIC NAME:
Clupea harengus

Sockeye salmon

Sockeye salmon live in the ocean until they are two to four years old. Then they enter rivers and swim to the breeding grounds where they were hatched, sometimes as far as 1,000 miles inland. After laying their eggs, the adult salmon die.

FOUND IN:
Pacific Ocean

SIZE:
Up to 33 in long

SCIENTIFIC NAME:
Oncorhynchus nerka

Dolphinfish

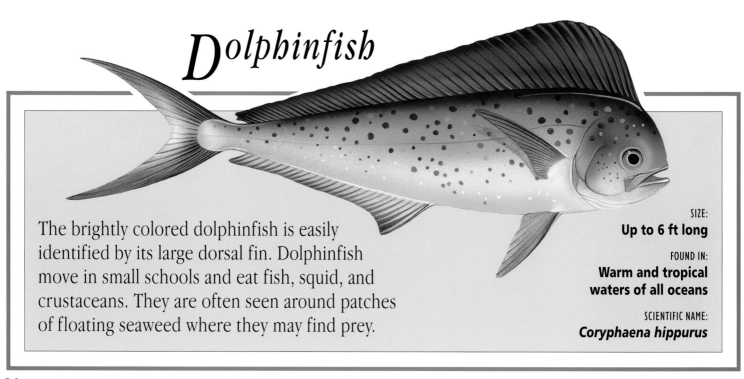

The brightly colored dolphinfish is easily identified by its large dorsal fin. Dolphinfish move in small schools and eat fish, squid, and crustaceans. They are often seen around patches of floating seaweed where they may find prey.

SIZE:
Up to 6 ft long

FOUND IN:
Warm and tropical waters of all oceans

SCIENTIFIC NAME:
Coryphaena hippurus

Haddock

FOUND IN:
North Atlantic Ocean

SIZE:
30–44 in long

SCIENTIFIC NAME:
Melanogrammus aeglefinus

The haddock is a member of the cod family and feeds on fish, crustaceans, and other marine life. It gathers in shoals to spawn and the eggs are left to float in the surface waters until they hatch into larvae.

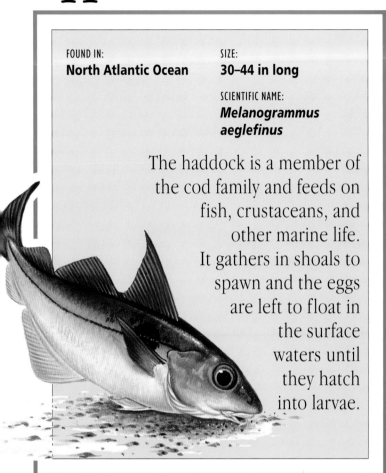

Atlantic mackerel

FOUND IN:
Atlantic Ocean and Mediterranean Sea

SIZE:
16–26 in long

SCIENTIFIC NAME:
Scomber scombrus

Mackerel move in large schools and make regular migration journeys. In spring and summer they go north, where they breed, and then they return south again in winter. Adult mackerel eat small fish and crustaceans, while young fish feed mainly on plankton and fish larvae.

Oarfish

This unusual fish has a long, ribbonlike body with a fin running along most of its length. It swims with rippling, serpentine movements. The oarfish has no teeth in its small mouth and eats shrimplike crustaceans.

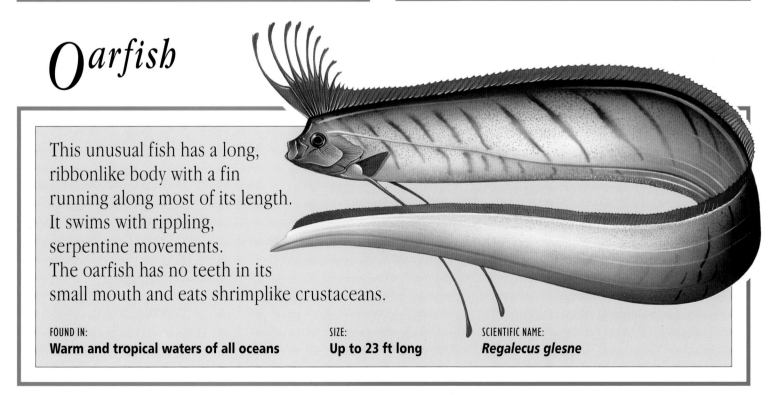

FOUND IN:
Warm and tropical waters of all oceans

SIZE:
Up to 23 ft long

SCIENTIFIC NAME:
Regalecus glesne

FOCUS ON: *Tuna fish*

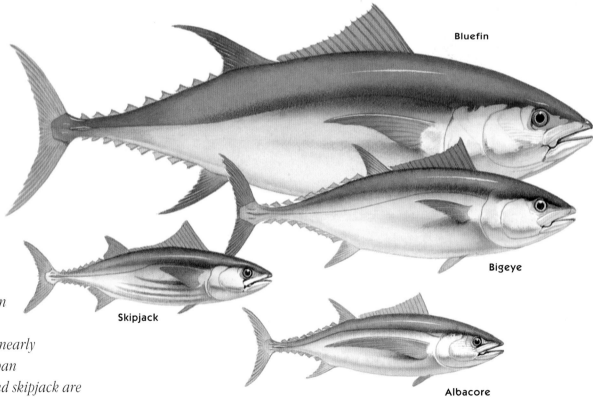

Among the fastest of all fish, tunas are shaped for speed and can swim at 50 miles an hour or more. They are the most streamlined fish, with a pointed head and a torpedo-shaped body tapering to a narrow tail stalk and crescent tail.

The 13 different species of tuna live in the surface waters of warm and tropical oceans. All are hunters feeding mainly on fish and squid. Many swim in large schools, but the biggest fish usually swim in smaller groups or alone. Groups of tuna have been seen herding schools of smaller fish before attacking them.

Tuna rarely, if ever, stop swimming because they have to swim to breathe. They swim with their mouths open so there is a constant flow of water over the gills. Fish obtain oxygen from water, not air; the oxygen is taken out of the water flowing past the gills. Most fish have to pump water over the gills by muscle action in order to obtain oxygen. Tuna, however, must keep swimming at all times to create a constant flow of water over the gills. The faster the tuna swims, the more water passes over the gills and the more oxygen can be removed.

Bluefin

Skipjack

Bigeye

Albacore

Types of tuna

The bluefin is the biggest of the tuna. It can grow up to 10 feet long and weigh more than 1,200 pounds—as much as seven or eight people. The bluefin has been known to cross the Atlantic in 119 days.

The bigeye tuna grows to nearly 8 feet and can weigh more than 400 pounds. The albacore and skipjack are smaller—up to 5 feet and 3 feet respectively.

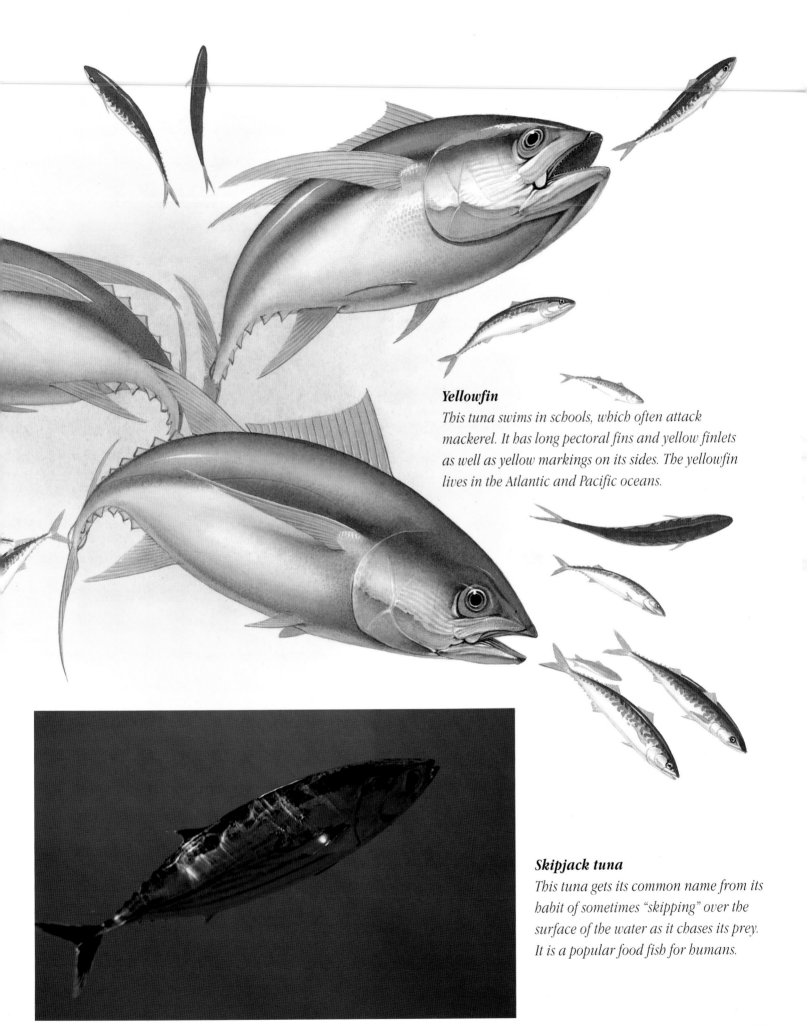

Yellowfin

This tuna swims in schools, which often attack
mackerel. It has long pectoral fins and yellow finlets
as well as yellow markings on its sides. The yellowfin
lives in the Atlantic and Pacific oceans.

Skipjack tuna

This tuna gets its common name from its
habit of sometimes "skipping" over the
surface of the water as it chases its prey.
It is a popular food fish for humans.

Purple jellyfish

Like most jellyfish, this creature has many stinging cells on its long tentacles. These cells protect it from enemies and help it to catch plankton to eat. Although known as the purple jellyfish, it may be yellow, red, or even brown in color.

FOUND IN:
Atlantic, Indian, and Pacific oceans

SIZE:
**Bell: 4 in wide
Tentacles: 3 ft long**

SCIENTIFIC NAME:
Pelagia noctiluca

Goose barnacles

FOUND IN:
Atlantic and Pacific oceans

SIZE:
6 in, including stalk

SCIENTIFIC NAME:
Lepas anatifera

Goose barnacles live fixed by their stalks to any object floating in the open sea, including logs and buoys as well as boats. The barnacle's body is enclosed by a shell made of five plates. These open at the top so that the barnacle can extend its six pairs of feathery arms and collect tiny particles of food from the water.

Squid

FOUND IN:
Atlantic Ocean and Mediterranean Sea

SIZE:
Up to 30 in long, including tentacles

SCIENTIFIC NAME:
Loligo pealii

The squid has a long, torpedo-shaped body, four pairs of arms, and one pair of much longer tentacles. Suckers on the arms and the tips of the tentacles help the squid grasp its prey—mostly fish and crustaceans. A fast swimmer, the squid moves by a type of jet propulsion, shooting water out of its body to force itself backward through the water.

Portuguese man-of-war

FOUND IN:
Warm and tropical waters in Atlantic, Indian, and Pacific oceans

SIZE:
Float: 12 in long
Tentacles: up to 60 ft

SCIENTIFIC NAME:
Physalia physalis

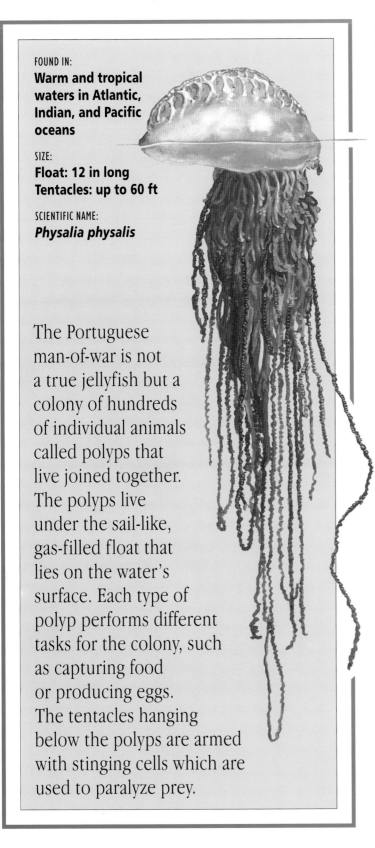

The Portuguese man-of-war is not a true jellyfish but a colony of hundreds of individual animals called polyps that live joined together. The polyps live under the sail-like, gas-filled float that lies on the water's surface. Each type of polyp performs different tasks for the colony, such as capturing food or producing eggs. The tentacles hanging below the polyps are armed with stinging cells which are used to paralyze prey.

Purple sea snail

FOUND IN:
Atlantic, Indian, and Pacific oceans

SIZE:
1 in long

SCIENTIFIC NAME:
Janthina janthina

This little snail cannot swim, but it drifts in the surface waters of the sea clinging to a raft of bubbles. These bubbles are made from mucus secreted from the snail's body that hardens when it enters the water.

Common comb jelly

FOUND IN:
Arctic and Atlantic oceans

SIZE:
6 in high

SCIENTIFIC NAME:
Bolinopsis infundibulum

The comb jelly moves with the help of tiny hairs arranged in lines down its baglike body. These hairs are called comb plates and they beat together to push the comb jelly through the water.

Focus on: *Marine turtles*

These great turtles are among the few reptiles that live in the ocean. With their flippers beating like wings they glide gracefully through the warm waters of the Atlantic, Pacific, and Indian oceans.

There are eight different species of marine turtle. All have long flippers, beaklike jaws, and an upper and lower shell to protect their soft body. They spend most of their time under the water, but they must come to the surface at regular intervals to breathe.

Males rarely leave the sea, but females come ashore to lay their eggs in pits which they dig on a sandy beach. Many turtles migrate hundreds of miles across the sea from feeding grounds to the beach of their birth to lay eggs. Green turtles that feed off the coast of Brazil travel some 870 miles to Ascension Island in the mid-Atlantic.

Hawksbill

Hawksbills have long been hunted for their beautiful shells as well as for their eggs. There are now strict controls on hunting but numbers of hawksbill turtles are still low. The hawksbill has an unusual diet. As well as eating mollusks and crustaceans, it feeds on sponges, many of which contain poisonous substances. The poisons do not seem to affect the turtles.

Olive ridley nesting

The ridley turtles are the smallest marine turtles—the olive ridley grows up to about 28 inches long. Olive ridleys travel to various nesting sites, including ones in Mexico, Costa Rica, and India.

Once she reaches the nest site, the female turtle struggles up the beach where she digs a pit and lays a clutch of about 100 eggs. This takes her just under an hour. She then covers the eggs with sand and returns to the sea. The eggs incubate in

the pit for up to 65 days. When the baby turtles hatch, they must dig their own way to the surface and head down the beach to the sea. Sadly, many are taken by birds and other predators before they reach the water.

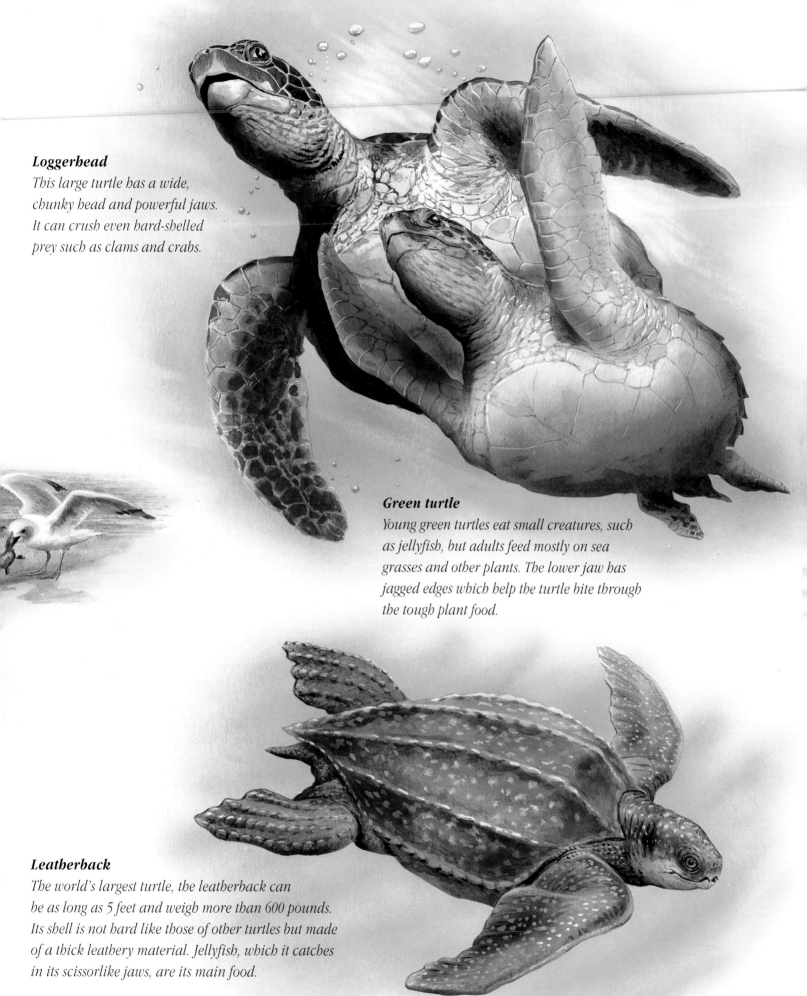

Loggerhead

This large turtle has a wide, chunky head and powerful jaws. It can crush even hard-shelled prey such as clams and crabs.

Green turtle

Young green turtles eat small creatures, such as jellyfish, but adults feed mostly on sea grasses and other plants. The lower jaw has jagged edges which help the turtle bite through the tough plant food.

Leatherback

The world's largest turtle, the leatherback can be as long as 5 feet and weigh more than 600 pounds. Its shell is not hard like those of other turtles but made of a thick leathery material. Jellyfish, which it catches in its scissorlike jaws, are its main food.

Great frigate bird

Frigate birds spend most of their lives in the air and feed by snatching fish from the water's surface. Males have red throat pouches, which they puff up during courtship displays.

FOUND IN:
Tropical waters of Indian and Pacific oceans

SIZE:
Body: 37–43 in

SCIENTIFIC NAME:
Fregata minor

Common dolphin

FOUND IN:
Warm and tropical waters in Atlantic, Indian, and Pacific oceans

SIZE:
7–8½ ft long

SCIENTIFIC NAME:
Delphinus delphis

Blue whale

The blue whale is probably the largest animal that has ever lived, bigger than the biggest dinosaurs. Despite its huge size its body is streamlined and moves gracefully in the water. This giant feeds entirely on plankton, in particular the shrimplike creatures called krill, which it filters from the water.

FOUND IN:
All oceans

SIZE:
Up to 100 ft long

SCIENTIFIC NAME:
Balaeonoptera musculus

Red-tailed tropic bird

Tropic birds fly far over tropical oceans. They catch fish and squid by hovering above the water and then plunging down to grab their prey.

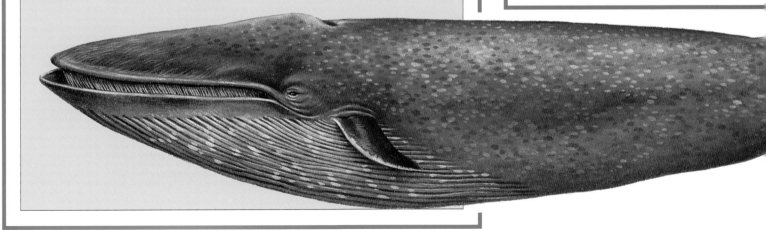

Humpback whale

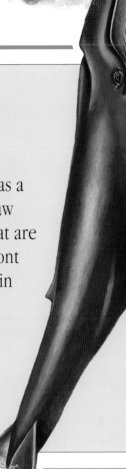

The dolphin is a small whale. It has a slender, streamlined body, a bulging forehead, and a beaked snout. A fast and agile swimmer, it can stay under the water for several minutes while hunting prey.

FOUND IN:
All oceans

SIZE:
50–60 ft long

SCIENTIFIC NAME:
Megaptera novaeangliae

The humpback whale has a strongly curved lower jaw and unusual flippers that are scalloped along their front edges. Humpbacks live in family groups and communicate with one another in long, complex songs which may be repeated for hours on end.

FOUND IN:
Indian and Pacific oceans

SIZE:
Body: 16 in long; tail 20 in

SCIENTIFIC NAME:
Phaethon rubricauda

Dall's porpoise

FOUND IN:
North Pacific Ocean

SIZE:
6–7½ ft long

SCIENTIFIC NAME:
Phocoenides dalli

This heavy-bodied porpoise lives in family groups of 15 to 20 animals. The groups sometimes gather in schools of up to 100 when migrating north in summer and south in winter. Dall's porpoise is a fast swimmer and is seen farther out to sea than most porpoises.

Seabed

The hidden world of the seabed is home to creatures as different as sponges and sharks.

In the shallow seas close to land, where the water is rarely more than 650 feet deep, there is plenty of life on the seabed. The bottom itself may be rock, fine sand, or mud; animals live on or close to the seabed or hide in the sediment.

A constant rain of dead plant and animal matter sinks down to the seabed from surface waters. Animal plankton and other small creatures feed on this matter, but some also settles into the sand or mud. Here it is consumed by creatures such as tiny worms and shrimps that live among the sediment. All of these creatures provide food for larger seabed inhabitants.

Some crabs, shrimps, and fish spend much of their lives hidden in burrows in the seabed, only leaving them to search for prey. Other creatures, such as sea pens and sponges, live permanently attached to the seabed and filter tiny items of food from the surrounding water. Flatfish, such as flounders and sole, are perfectly adapted to lie partly hidden in the sand, while keeping a watchful eye out for a passing meal.

There are bigger creatures, too. The carpet shark, for example, has a body edged with flaps and frills. These, as its name suggests, make it look much like an old rug as it lies on the seabed watching for prey.

Colonies of sea squirts, or tunicates, live on the seabed, where they filter tiny items of food from the water.

Goosefish

Also known as the angler, this fish is fringed with flaps of skin that help it stay hidden on the seabed. Above its mouth is a spine tipped with a flap of skin that acts as a lure—other fish think it might be a tasty piece of food. When they come close, the angler snaps them up.

FOUND IN:
Atlantic Ocean and Mediterranean Sea

SIZE:
2–6 ft long

SCIENTIFIC NAME:
Lophius americanus

Northern sea robin

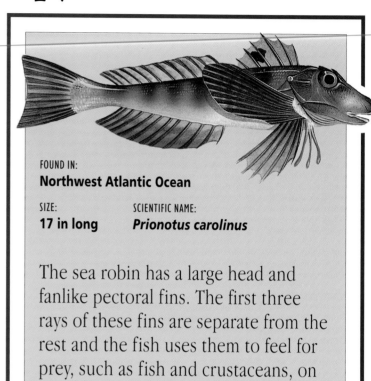

FOUND IN:
Northwest Atlantic Ocean

SIZE:
17 in long

SCIENTIFIC NAME:
Prionotus carolinus

The sea robin has a large head and fanlike pectoral fins. The first three rays of these fins are separate from the rest and the fish uses them to feel for prey, such as fish and crustaceans, on the seabed. If in danger the sea robin buries itself in sand, leaving only the top of its head and its eyes exposed.

Hagfish

The hagfish spends much of its life burrowed into soft mud on the seabed. It has no jaws, just a slitlike mouth surrounded by small tentacles. It has no scales on its body and is almost blind, although its senses of smell and touch are good. The hagfish eats crustaceans, but it also feeds on dead and dying fish. Using its toothed tongue, the hagfish bores into the prey's body and eats away all its flesh.

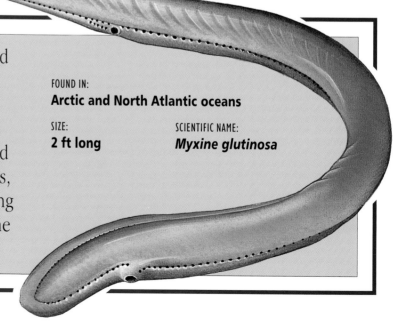

FOUND IN:
Arctic and North Atlantic oceans

SIZE:
2 ft long

SCIENTIFIC NAME:
Myxine glutinosa

Sandy dogfish

FOUND IN:
North Atlantic Ocean

SIZE:
2–3 ft long

SCIENTIFIC NAME:
Scyliorhinus canicula

Dogfish are small sharks. This species lives on sandy and muddy seabeds, where it feeds on fish and many kinds of bottom-living creatures, such as crabs, mollusks, and worms.

Greenland shark

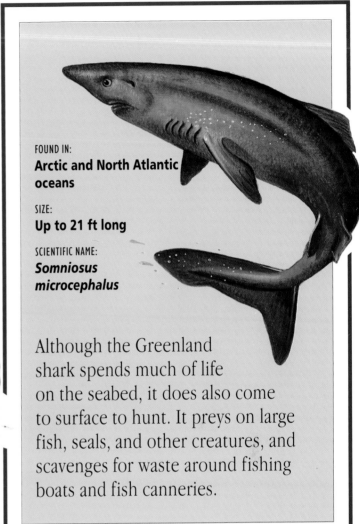

FOUND IN:
Arctic and North Atlantic oceans

SIZE:
Up to 21 ft long

SCIENTIFIC NAME:
Somniosus microcephalus

Although the Greenland shark spends much of life on the seabed, it does also come to surface to hunt. It preys on large fish, seals, and other creatures, and scavenges for waste around fishing boats and fish canneries.

Ocean pout

This fish belongs to the family known as eelpouts. It lives on the seabed, feeding on creatures such as crabs and urchins. In the fall, it moves to deeper waters to spawn. One female may lay 4,000 eggs, which lie on the bottom until they hatch two or three months later.

FOUND IN:
North Atlantic Ocean

SIZE:
3½ ft long

SCIENTIFIC NAME:
Macrozoarces americanus

43

FOCUS ON: *Skates, rays, and seabed sharks*

There are more than 300 different species of skates and rays found worldwide. Most have an extremely broad flattened body and huge winglike fins, giving them a diamond shape. As they swim, the fish flap their fins up and down, and appear almost to be flying through the water. Skates and rays spend much of their lives on or near the seabed. Their flattened bodies make them hard to see as they lie half-covered with sand. Small openings, called spiracles, on the upper surface of the head allow them to breathe as they lie on the seabed. They feed mostly on mollusks, crustaceans, and fish and also scavenge any dead creatures and other waste that falls to the sea floor.

Sharks are usually thought of as being fast swimmers in surface waters, but some are seabed dwellers. Horn sharks, nurse sharks, and carpet sharks lurk on the bottom much of the time, moving only to catch passing prey.

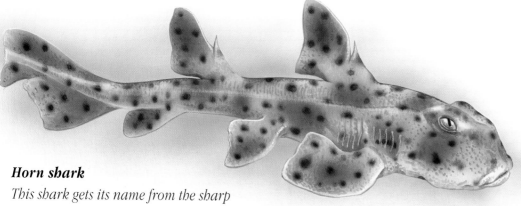

Carpet shark
Camouflaged by its coloring and many flaps of skin, the carpet shark lies on the seabed waiting for prey to come near.

Horn shark
This shark gets its name from the sharp spines in front of the fins on its back. Active at night, it collects prey such as sea urchins, crabs, and worms on the seabed.

Skate
The skate's flattened body is covered with tiny spines and a line of larger spines runs down the middle of the tail. The spines help the skate defend itself against attackers.

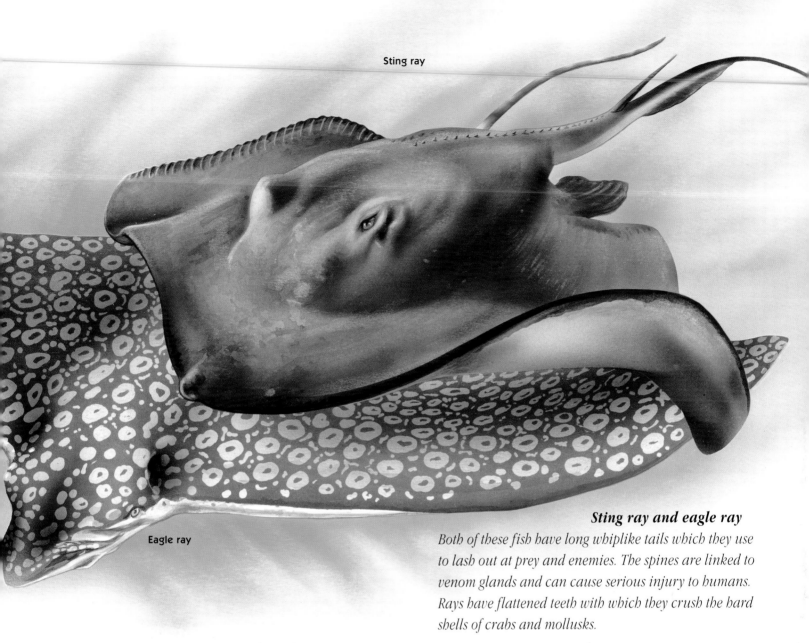

Sting ray

Eagle ray

Sting ray and eagle ray

Both of these fish have long whiplike tails which they use to lash out at prey and enemies. The spines are linked to venom glands and can cause serious injury to humans. Rays have flattened teeth with which they crush the hard shells of crabs and mollusks.

Nurse shark

A slow-moving bottom dweller, the nurse shark has lots of short, sharp teeth, ideal for crushing shellfish. The sensitive fleshy whiskers on its flattened head are thought to help it find hidden prey on the seabed.

45

Turbot

This extremely broad-bodied flatfish varies in color, but it usually has speckled markings that help to keep it hidden as it lies on the seabed. Adult turbots feed mostly on fish but young turbots eat crustaceans.

FOUND IN:
East Atlantic Ocean and Mediterranean Sea

SIZE:
3 ft long

SCIENTIFIC NAME:
Psetta maxima

Naked sole

The naked sole has no scales on its skin and is marked with dark stripes on the uppermost side. Both its eyes are positioned on this side. It is an active hunter and can swim well when necessary.

FOUND IN:
Northwest Atlantic Ocean

SIZE:
6–9 in long

SCIENTIFIC NAME:
Gymnachirus melas

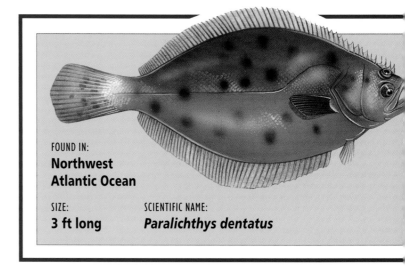

FOUND IN:
Northwest Atlantic Ocean

SIZE:
3 ft long

SCIENTIFIC NAME:
Paralichthys dentatus

Toadfish

The bottom-dwelling toadfish has a large, slightly flattened head, with eyes near the top. On its body are rows of light-producing organs, called photophores, each of which shines as the fish lies on the dark seabed. The toadfish preys on mollusks and crustaceans.

C^{od}

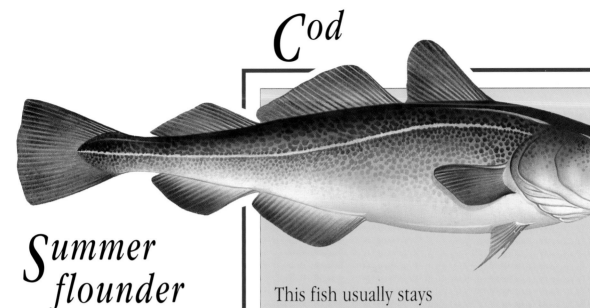

S^{ummer} flounder

This fish usually stays near the bottom, but it also searches for prey, such as mollusks and other fish, near the surface. On its chin is a fleshy projection called a barbel. This may help the cod feel for prey hidden in the seabed. The cod is an important source of food for humans, and millions are caught every year.

FOUND IN:	SIZE:	SCIENTIFIC NAME:
North Atlantic Ocean	**Up to 6 ft long**	*Gadus morhua*

This typical flatfish has a flattened body with both eyes on one side. Like most flatfish, this flounder spends much of its life lying half-buried on the seabed, eyed side upward. It will swim to the surface if chasing prey.

$A^{tlantic}$ torpedo

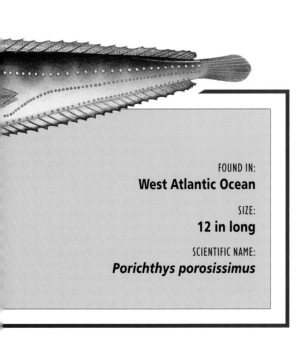

FOUND IN:
West Atlantic Ocean

SIZE:
12 in long

SCIENTIFIC NAME:
Porichthys porosissimus

FOUND IN:
Atlantic Ocean

SIZE:
Up to 6 ft long

SCIENTIFIC NAME:
Torpedo nobiliana

This fish has special muscles in its body which it uses to produce electric charges of up to 220 volts. This is powerful enough to stun prey and would give a severe shock to a person.

Clam

The usual home of the clam is a burrow deep in a sandy or muddy seabed. The clam digs its burrow with a fleshy part of its body called the foot. Long tubes extend from the shell so that the clam can take in tiny living particles to eat and water to get oxygen.

FOUND IN:
North Pacific Ocean

SIZE:
6 in long

SCIENTIFIC NAME:
Saxidomus nuttalli

Scallop

FOUND IN:
Atlantic and Pacific oceans

SIZE:
4 in long

SCIENTIFIC NAME:
Chlamys islandicus

The scallop has a soft body protected by two shells. A row of well-developed eyes can be seen when the shells are slightly parted. The scallop moves by flapping its shells together, forcing out jets of water which push it forward.

Sea pen

The featherlike sea pen is not one animal but a group of many individuals called polyps living together. One large stemlike polyp stands embedded in the mud or sand of the seabed and supports the whole group. On the side branches there are many small white feeding polyps. If touched, the sea pen gleams with phosphorescence.

FOUND IN:
North Atlantic Ocean

SIZE:
Up to 15 in high

SCIENTIFIC NAME:
Pennatula phosphorea

Lightning whelk

This large whelk has a very beautiful spiral shell with brown markings. It lives on sandy or muddy seabeds in shallow water and feeds mostly on other mollusks, such as clams, which it digs up.

FOUND IN:
Atlantic Ocean

SIZE:
16 in long

SCIENTIFIC NAME:
Busycon contrarium

Sponge

Sponges are among the simplest of animals. To feed, they draw water into the chambers of the body where tiny particles of food are trapped and digested.

FOUND IN:
Caribbean Sea

SIZE:
Up to 20 in long

SCIENTIFIC NAME:
Callyspongia spp.

Sea cucumber

Sea cucumbers are related to starfish, but they have long simple bodies. At one end is the anus and at the other the mouth, which is surrounded by food-gathering tentacles. Rows of tiny tube feet run the length of the body. When disturbed, the sea cucumber ejects sticky white threads from its anus. These confuse predators.

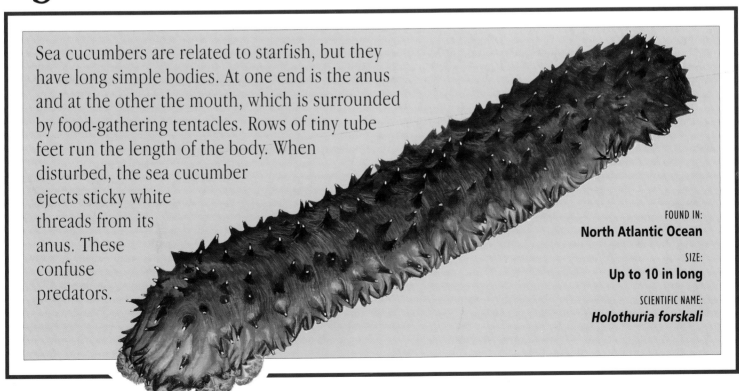

FOUND IN:
North Atlantic Ocean

SIZE:
Up to 10 in long

SCIENTIFIC NAME:
Holothuria forskali

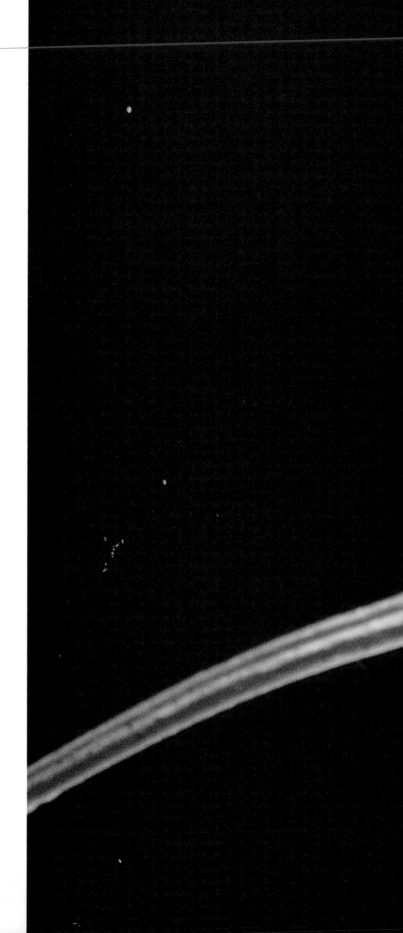

Deep sea

Fish with glowing lights on their bodies are just some of the strange creatures that live in the cold, dark waters of the deep sea.

The deep-sea zone begins at about 650 feet. From this depth down to about 3,300 feet—the twilight zone—some light filters through the water, but below 3,300 feet the ocean is totally dark. No light can reach these depths. Plants depend on light so no plants can survive here. Creatures in the deepest sea must live by hunting each other or scavenging whatever food drifts down from above. The deep sea is cold, too—generally about 32°F.

Despite the cold, dark conditions some creatures have adapted to life in the deep sea. Life is much sparser here than elsewhere in the ocean, so the inhabitants have developed ways to help them find food and others of their kind to mate with. Many deep-sea fish, such as gulper eels and viperfish, have large mouths for their body size. This helps them gulp down any prey that does appear. Other deep-sea animals are very sensitive to the slightest movement in the water. Deep-sea shrimp, for example, have extra-long antennae, which they spread out in the water to help them detect prey.

Some creatures, such as hatchetfish, even carry their own light sources. Light-producing organs arranged in rows on their bodies help them to attract mates or confuse predators. In many of these fish the light is made by chemical reactions inside the light organs.

The dragonfish, with its large jaws and gleaming light organs, is typical of the curious creatures that lurk in the deep sea.

Football fish

This unusual fish has a round body studded with bony plates, each with a central spine. On its head is a "fishing rod," or lure, which carries a light-producing organ. It uses this lure to attract prey in the darkness of the deep sea.

FOUND IN:
All oceans

SIZE:
2 ft long

SCIENTIFIC NAME:
Himantolophus groenlandicus

Gulper eel

Tripod fish

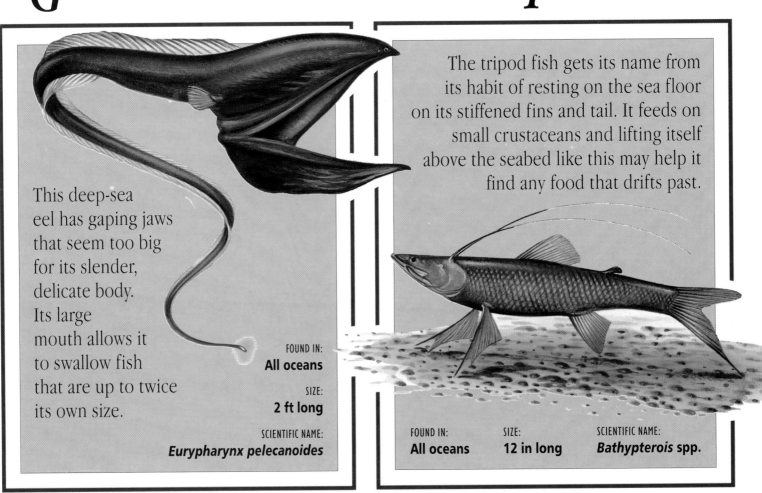

This deep-sea eel has gaping jaws that seem too big for its slender, delicate body. Its large mouth allows it to swallow fish that are up to twice its own size.

FOUND IN:
All oceans

SIZE:
2 ft long

SCIENTIFIC NAME:
Eurypharynx pelecanoides

The tripod fish gets its name from its habit of resting on the sea floor on its stiffened fins and tail. It feeds on small crustaceans and lifting itself above the seabed like this may help it find any food that drifts past.

FOUND IN:
All oceans

SIZE:
12 in long

SCIENTIFIC NAME:
Bathypterois spp.

Viperfish

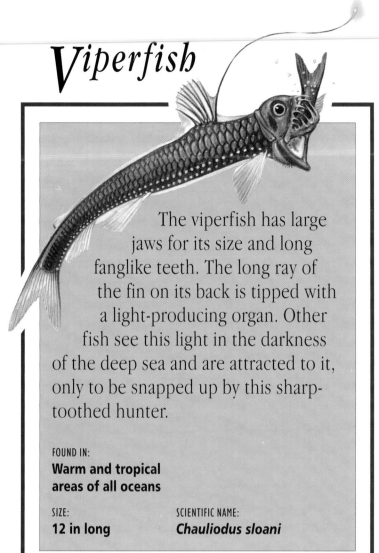

The viperfish has large jaws for its size and long fanglike teeth. The long ray of the fin on its back is tipped with a light-producing organ. Other fish see this light in the darkness of the deep sea and are attracted to it, only to be snapped up by this sharp-toothed hunter.

FOUND IN:
Warm and tropical areas of all oceans

SIZE:
12 in long

SCIENTIFIC NAME:
Chauliodus sloani

Hatchetfish

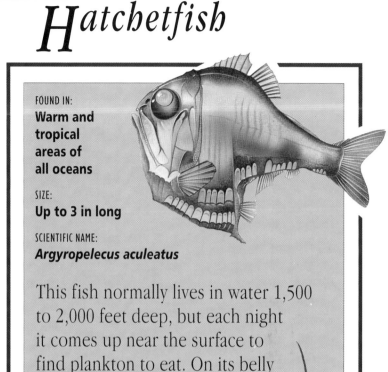

FOUND IN:
Warm and tropical areas of all oceans

SIZE:
Up to 3 in long

SCIENTIFIC NAME:
Argyropelecus aculeatus

This fish normally lives in water 1,500 to 2,000 feet deep, but each night it comes up near the surface to find plankton to eat. On its belly are rows of light-producing organs, which give out a pale blue light. This confuses predators about the size and shape of the fish's body, making it harder to catch.

Ratfish

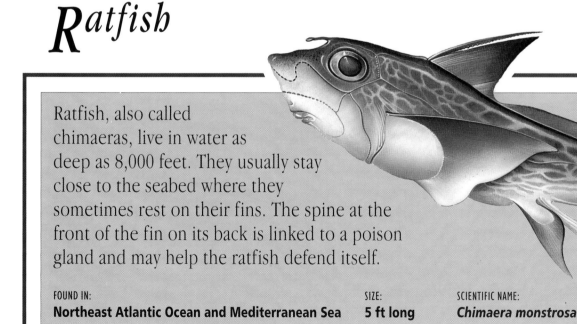

Ratfish, also called chimaeras, live in water as deep as 8,000 feet. They usually stay close to the seabed where they sometimes rest on their fins. The spine at the front of the fin on its back is linked to a poison gland and may help the ratfish defend itself.

FOUND IN:
Northeast Atlantic Ocean and Mediterranean Sea

SIZE:
5 ft long

SCIENTIFIC NAME:
Chimaera monstrosa

FOCUS ON: *Sperm whales*

The deepest divers of all whales, sperm whales regularly go down to 3,300 feet. They can remain underwater for 45 minutes or more as they hunt for food such as giant squid.

The huge square head of the sperm whale contains a mass of a waxy substance called spermaceti. Scientists are not sure about the function of this substance, but one theory is that it helps the whale dive to great depths. As the whale dives, cold water in the nasal passages in the head cools and solidifies the wax. This makes the head more dense and helps the whale to descend. When the whale comes up again, blood flow is increased and the wax is warmed by surrounding blood vessels and becomes more liquid. This makes the whale more buoyant so it is easier for it to return to the surface.

A mighty tail
As a sperm whale begins a dive, it lifts its great tail above the surface. Each tail has its own pattern of nicks and scars which help whale watchers identify individuals. Once under the water, the whale travels into the depths at a speed of up to 5 miles per hour.

The long journey
The largest of the toothed whales, the sperm whale grows up to 50 feet long. Its head, with its huge upper jaw and much smaller lower jaw, is about one third of its total length. Sperm whales generally spend the winter months in warm waters near the equator, where they breed. In spring they migrate toward the poles where they remain for the summer.

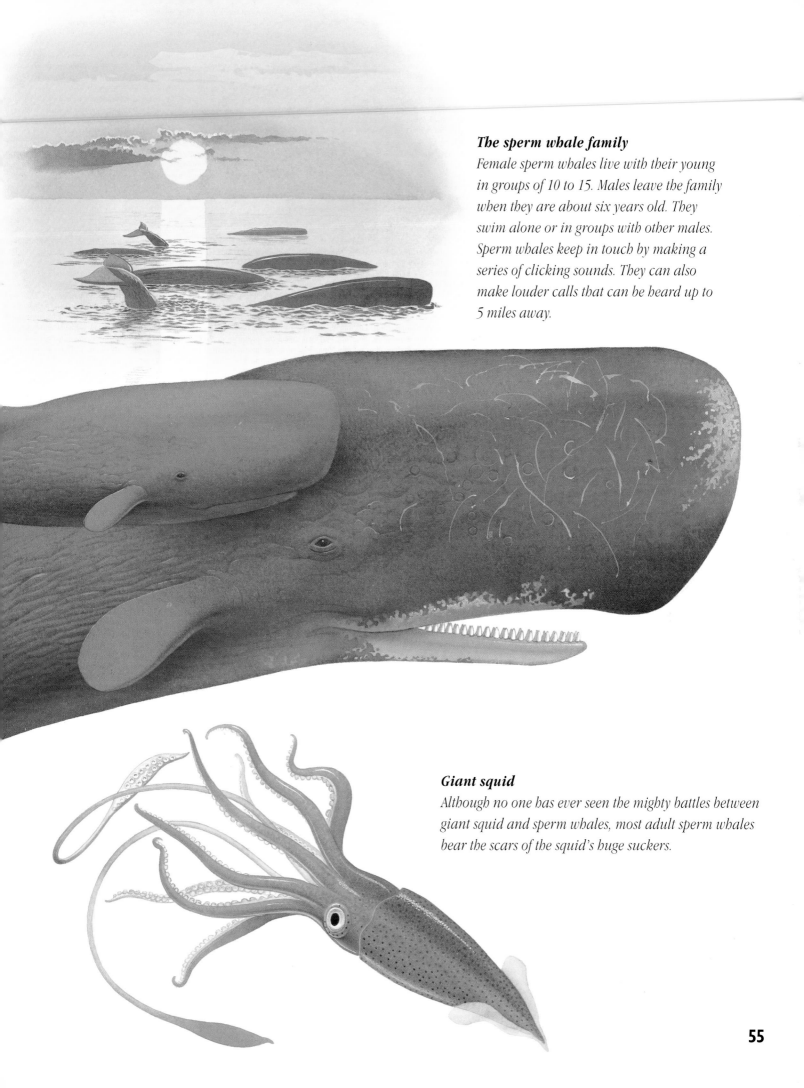

The sperm whale family

Female sperm whales live with their young in groups of 10 to 15. Males leave the family when they are about six years old. They swim alone or in groups with other males. Sperm whales keep in touch by making a series of clicking sounds. They can also make louder calls that can be heard up to 5 miles away.

Giant squid

Although no one has ever seen the mighty battles between giant squid and sperm whales, most adult sperm whales bear the scars of the squid's huge suckers.

*S*ea lily

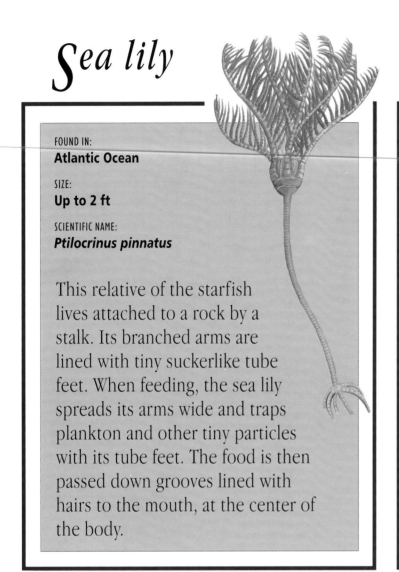

FOUND IN:
Atlantic Ocean

SIZE:
Up to 2 ft

SCIENTIFIC NAME:
Ptilocrinus pinnatus

This relative of the starfish lives attached to a rock by a stalk. Its branched arms are lined with tiny suckerlike tube feet. When feeding, the sea lily spreads its arms wide and traps plankton and other tiny particles with its tube feet. The food is then passed down grooves lined with hairs to the mouth, at the center of the body.

*L*ampshell

The lampshell belongs to a group of animals called brachiopods, which has lived on Earth for 600 million years. It has two shells and a short stalk on which it can move around. When the shells gape open they expose folded tentacles lined with tiny hairs. These hairs drive water over the tentacles where tiny particles of food are trapped.

FOUND IN:
Atlantic Ocean

SIZE:
1¼ in long

SCIENTIFIC NAME:
Terebratulina septentrionalis

*D*eep-sea shrimp

Deep-sea shrimp have antennae longer than their bodies to help them find food in the dark waters. They eat any dead and decaying matter that they can find.

FOUND IN:
Atlantic Ocean

SIZE:
4 in long

SCIENTIFIC NAME:
***Pasiphaea* spp.**

Nautilus

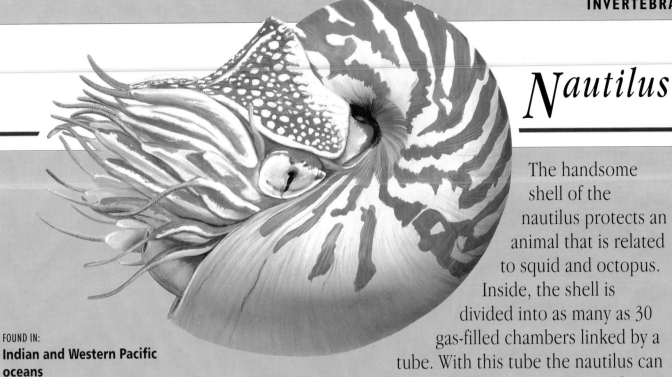

The handsome shell of the nautilus protects an animal that is related to squid and octopus. Inside, the shell is divided into as many as 30 gas-filled chambers linked by a tube. With this tube the nautilus can alter the amount of gas in each chamber to make itself rise or sink in the water. It generally lives in deep water below 650 feet, where it preys on crabs and other crustaceans.

FOUND IN:
Indian and Western Pacific oceans

SIZE:
8 in long

SCIENTIFIC NAME:
Nautilus nautilus

Brittle star

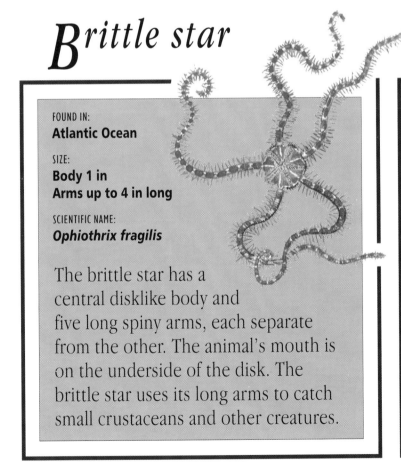

FOUND IN:
Atlantic Ocean

SIZE:
Body 1 in
Arms up to 4 in long

SCIENTIFIC NAME:
Ophiothrix fragilis

The brittle star has a central disklike body and five long spiny arms, each separate from the other. The animal's mouth is on the underside of the disk. The brittle star uses its long arms to catch small crustaceans and other creatures.

Glass sponge

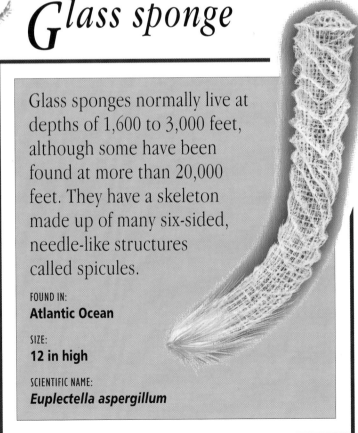

Glass sponges normally live at depths of 1,600 to 3,000 feet, although some have been found at more than 20,000 feet. They have a skeleton made up of many six-sided, needle-like structures called spicules.

FOUND IN:
Atlantic Ocean

SIZE:
12 in high

SCIENTIFIC NAME:
Euplectella aspergillum

Coral reefs

The rocky skeletons of thousands of tiny creatures make up a coral reef, home to some of the sea's most colorful creatures.

The world's coral reefs contain the richest variety of life in the oceans. They are made up of the skeletons of thousands of coral animals, relatives of the sea anemone. During their lives, the coral animals, called polyps, make hard skeletons around themselves. More and more of these skeletons build up on top of one another, forming a large structure called a coral reef.

A living polyp has a simple cuplike body with a single opening surrounded by tentacles. The polyp uses these tentacles, armed with stinging cells, to catch its food, which is then passed to the mouth in the center of the body. Because coral animals need warmth, they can only live in waters where the temperature is above 70° Fahrenheit. The water must also be clear—tiny marine plants live in the polyps and they need light in order to grow. The plants are essential to the coral—without them, the polyps cannot make their rocky skeletons.

A coral reef is also home to a great variety of other animals. Small fish, mollusks, and crustaceans feed on marine plants as well as the coral themselves. Larger fish come to the reef to find prey. Many coral reef fish are amazingly colorful. No one knows why this is so, but it may help the fish to recognize others of their own kind in a habitat where there is a bewildering variety of species.

Multicolored fish swim among the many different types of coral on this Indonesian reef.

Squirrelfish

After spending the day hiding in crevices in the reef, this fish comes out at night to hunt for small crustaceans and other prey. Its large eyes help it to see well in the dark.

FOUND IN:
Atlantic Ocean and Caribbean Sea

SIZE:
14 in long

SCIENTIFIC NAME:
Holocentrus ascensionis

Yellowtail snapper

Snappers are common around coral reefs and are a popular fish for humans to eat. This species is easily recognized by its bright yellow tail and the yellow stripe along each side. It feeds mostly on other fish and small crustaceans.

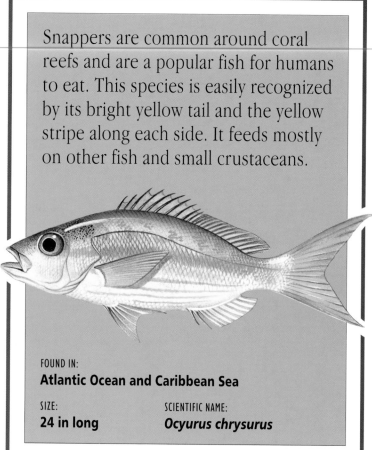

FOUND IN:
Atlantic Ocean and Caribbean Sea

SIZE:
24 in long

SCIENTIFIC NAME:
Ocyurus chrysurus

Queen angelfish

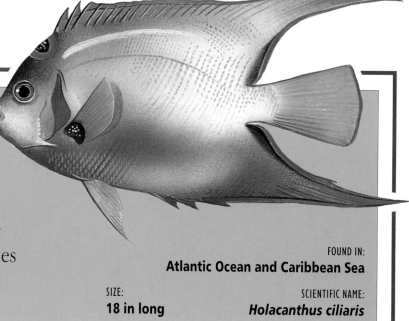

Despite its colorful markings, this angelfish can be hard to see among the bright corals. It has long fins on its back and belly, which extend past the tail fin. It feeds on sponges and other invertebrates. Young queen angelfish may act as cleaners—they pick and eat parasites off other fish.

FOUND IN:
Atlantic Ocean and Caribbean Sea

SIZE:
18 in long

SCIENTIFIC NAME:
Holacanthus ciliaris

Lionfish

With its brightly striped body and large fanlike fins, this fish is one of the most unusual on the reef. Spines in the fin on its back are extremely poisonous and can be dangerous even for humans. The fish uses its spines to defend itself, not to attack prey.

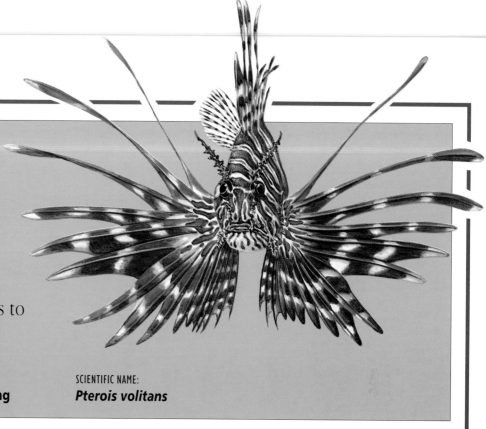

FOUND IN:
Indian and Pacific oceans

SIZE:
15 in long

SCIENTIFIC NAME:
Pterois volitans

Copperband butterfly fish

This fish uses its long beaklike snout to reach into crevices in the coral and find small creatures to eat. The large "eyespot" near its tail fin may confuse predators into thinking the copperband is larger than it is.

FOUND IN:
Indian and Pacific oceans

SIZE:
7 in long

SCIENTIFIC NAME:
Chelmon rostratus

Spangled emperor

The spangled emperor gets its name from the scattering of blue spots on its back and tail fins. It has a large head and thick lips, and feeds on other fish and invertebrates. Spangled emperors usually swim in small schools, each led by one large male.

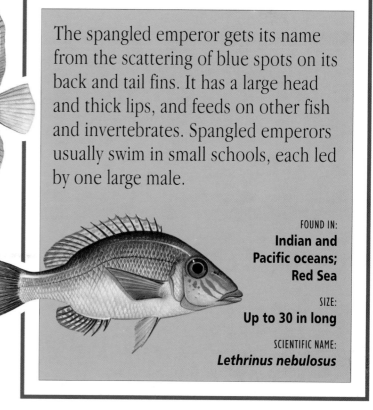

FOUND IN:
Indian and Pacific oceans; Red Sea

SIZE:
Up to 30 in long

SCIENTIFIC NAME:
Lethrinus nebulosus

FOCUS ON: Stony corals

The reef-building corals are called stony corals, or hard corals. They make a hard skeleton of calcium carbonate at the base of their bodies to protect themselves. Most of these corals form colonies, made as many polyps grow close to and even on top of one another. The colony quickly increases as new polyps bud from existing ones. The structure and size of these colonies vary from species to species, but fall into six main groups: there are branching fingerlike corals, brain corals, encrusting or boulder corals, leaf and sheet corals, fleshy corals, and flower and cup corals. Some stony corals, however, are solitary—they do not live in colonies. Individual polyps grow much larger than those of colonial corals.

During the day most polyps stay inside their rocky skeletons, called corallites. At night they extend their bodies and tentacles to catch food.

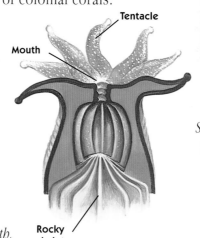

Tentacle

Mouth

Rocky skeleton

Polyp

Each coral polyp has a rocky skeleton at its base. The polyp itself has a ring of tentacles carrying stinging cells. The polyp catches food with its tentacles and passes it to its central mouth.

Lamarck's sheet coral

Sheet coral colonies form overlapping flattened plates. This species is most common in water between 65 and 120 feet deep and forms colonies up to 6 feet wide.

Smooth brain coral

This brain coral lives in colonies up to 4 feet wide and 2 feet high. It is most common in water 20 to 40 feet deep.

Mushroom coral

The fleshy mushroom coral lives on reefs at a depth of 30 to 250 feet in the Caribbean Sea and Atlantic Ocean around South Florida and the Bahamas. The single large polyps are up to 6 inches across and they have a rough texture.

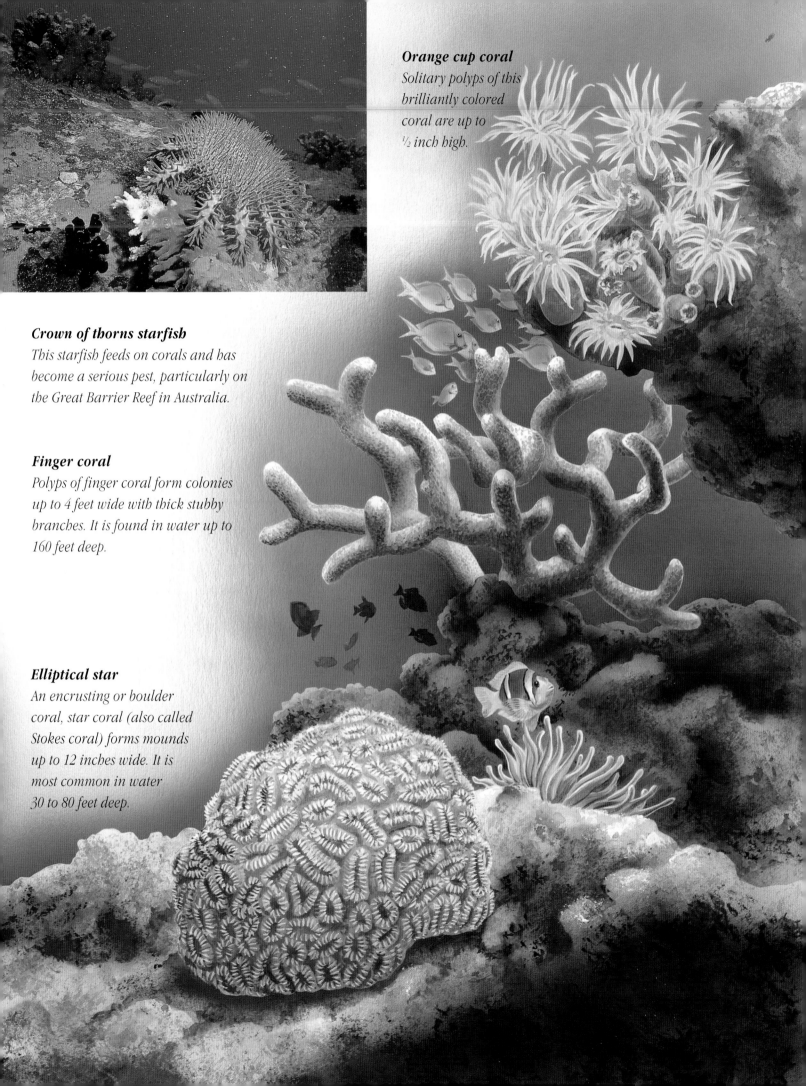

Orange cup coral
Solitary polyps of this brilliantly colored coral are up to ½ inch high.

Crown of thorns starfish
This starfish feeds on corals and has become a serious pest, particularly on the Great Barrier Reef in Australia.

Finger coral
Polyps of finger coral form colonies up to 4 feet wide with thick stubby branches. It is found in water up to 160 feet deep.

Elliptical star
An encrusting or boulder coral, star coral (also called Stokes coral) forms mounds up to 12 inches wide. It is most common in water 30 to 80 feet deep.

Clown anemonefish

This boldly striped fish lives among the tentacles of large sea anemones. It sometimes cleans waste from its host, and it may help to attract other fish that the anemone catches and eats. The anemone's stinging tentacles do not harm the anemonefish.

FOUND IN:
Pacific Ocean

SIZE:
2–3 in long

SCIENTIFIC NAME:
Amphiprion percula

Moorish idol

The beautiful moorish idol swims around the coral reef in pairs or small schools. It has a long snout, which helps it reach into crevices to feed on creatures such as sponges.

FOUND IN:
Indian and Pacific oceans

SIZE:
7 in

SCIENTIFIC NAME:
Zanclus cornutus

Barracuda

FOUND IN:
Atlantic Ocean and Caribbean Sea

SIZE:
Up to 6 ft long

SCIENTIFIC NAME:
Sphyraena barracuda

Barracudas are fierce predators common around coral reefs. They have sharp teeth and can be dangerous to humans if disturbed. Young barracudas often swim in schools, but larger fish generally hunt alone.

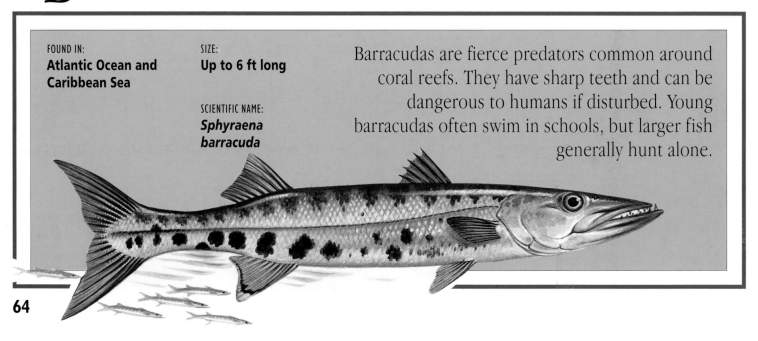

*Q*ueen *triggerfish*

FOUND IN:
West Atlantic Ocean and Caribbean Sea

SIZE:
22 in long

SCIENTIFIC NAME:
Balistes vetula

On the triggerfish's back are three spines. When the first spine is upright, it is locked into place by the second. If in danger, the triggerfish can wedge itself into a crevice with this "locking" spine and is extremely hard to move.

*B*lue parrot fish

As its name suggests, this fish has beaklike jaws. Its teeth are joined together to form strong plates, which it uses to scrape algae and coral off reefs. When young, these parrot fish are light blue. They turn darker blue as they get older.

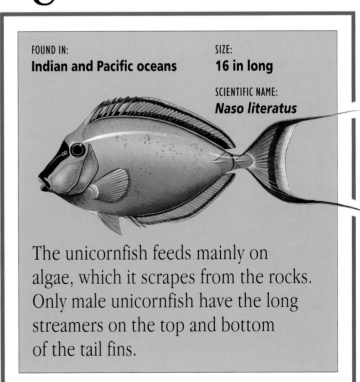

FOUND IN:
West Atlantic Ocean and Caribbean Sea

SIZE:
4 in long

SCIENTIFIC NAME:
Scarus coeruleus

*U*nicornfish

FOUND IN:
Indian and Pacific oceans

SIZE:
16 in long

SCIENTIFIC NAME:
Naso literatus

The unicornfish feeds mainly on algae, which it scrapes from the rocks. Only male unicornfish have the long streamers on the top and bottom of the tail fins.

Giant clam

This huge mollusk is the world's largest clam. Like other clams, it filters plankton from the water. It also has tiny algae living in its mantle—the tissue that lines the inside of the shell—which, like land plants, make sugars and starches by photosynthesis. The clam feeds on these nutrients.

FOUND IN:
Indian and Pacific oceans

SIZE:
3 ft wide

SCIENTIFIC NAME:
Tridacna gigas

Long-spined urchin

Sharp spines protect the urchin's rounded body from enemies. The urchin's mouth is on the underside of the body and has five teeth arranged in a circle for chewing food. By day these urchins stay hidden on the reef, but at night they come out to feed on algae.

Feather duster worm

The body of this spectacular worm usually remains hidden in a flexible tube attached to a reef or the seabed. The tube is made of fine sand stuck together with a gluey substance made in the worm's body. The worm catches food with its crown of feathery gills.

FOUND IN:
Atlantic Ocean and Caribbean Sea

SIZE:
5 in long

SCIENTIFIC NAME:
Sabellastarte magnifica

Sea fan

A sea fan is made up of a group of many tiny creatures called polyps. A gorgonian, or soft coral, it does not have a hard, reef-building skeleton like hard, or stony coral. The central "stem" and "branches" of the sea fan are made of a hornlike material and stay attached to rock. Polyps live on the "stem" and extend their tentacles to find food.

FOUND IN:
South Florida coast and Caribbean Sea

SIZE:
Up to 10 ft tall

SCIENTIFIC NAME:
***Gorgonia* spp.**

*T*horny starfish

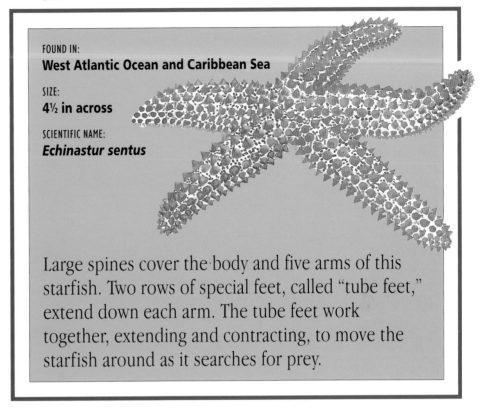

FOUND IN:
West Atlantic Ocean and Caribbean Sea

SIZE:
4½ in across

SCIENTIFIC NAME:
Echinastur sentus

Large spines cover the body and five arms of this starfish. Two rows of special feet, called "tube feet," extend down each arm. The tube feet work together, extending and contracting, to move the starfish around as it searches for prey.

FOUND IN:
Atlantic Ocean and Caribbean Sea

SIZE:
Body: 4 in wide; spines: 4–16 in long

SCIENTIFIC NAME:
Diadema antillarum

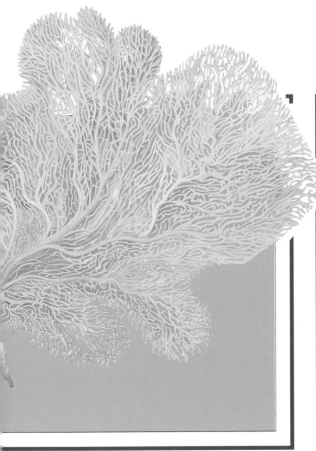

*A*tlantic deer cowrie

The cowrie is a type of sea snail with a beautiful shiny shell. Unlike most snails, the cowrie's mantle can be extended to cover the outside of the shell and camouflage the animal. The opening of the cowrie's shell is edged with 35 teeth.

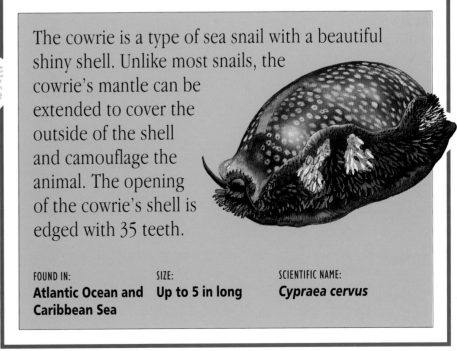

FOUND IN:
Atlantic Ocean and Caribbean Sea

SIZE:
Up to 5 in long

SCIENTIFIC NAME:
Cypraea cervus

polar seas

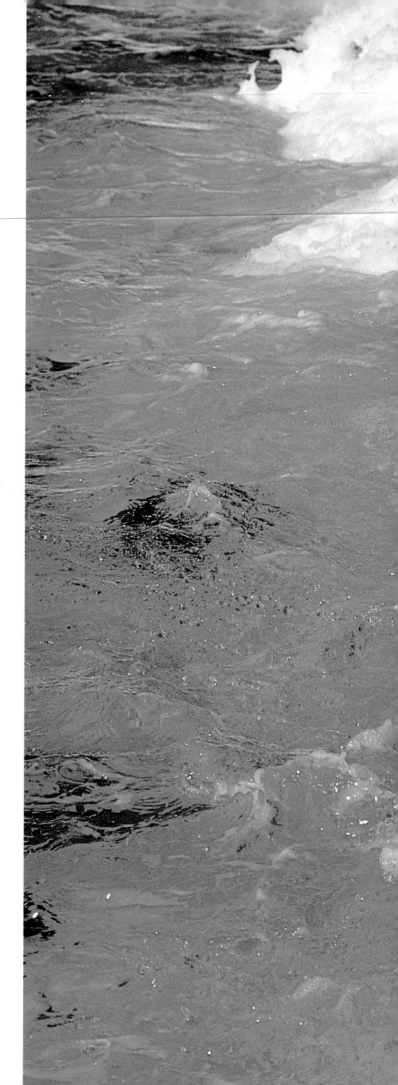

Even in the cold, icy waters of the Arctic and Antarctic, there is a wide variety of marine life.

The polar regions at the far north and south of the world are bitterly cold—cold enough to freeze seawater. In fact, most of the Arctic, the area around the North Pole, is a huge raft of ice. This frozen sea is called *pack ice*. The continent of Antarctica, the land around the South Pole, is also surrounded by floating ice. In winter, this extends 600 miles from the land.

Despite the cold and ice, polar seas teem with marine life. The waters are particularly rich in plankton. Polar fish thrive on the minute animals and plants, and also on each other. Over millions of years, these fish have adapted to the extreme cold. The Antarctic cod even has a special sort of antifreeze in its body which keeps its blood from turning to ice.

Polar waters are home to larger creatures, too. Many kinds of seals live in Arctic and Antarctic waters, and there are seven different species of penguin in the Antarctic. Some creatures only live in polar seas for part of the year. Great whales, such as the blue and the humpback, for example, spend summer months in the Antarctic feasting on plankton, and then travel toward the equator to give birth to their young in warmer waters. Seabirds, such as cormorants, petrels, and auks, fly to polar waters in summer to feed on the plentiful fish.

Millions of adélie penguins live and breed in Antarctica and search for their food in polar seas.

Antarctic krill

Shrimplike krill feed on tiny plant plankton. In turn they are the main food of many fish, penguins, and even whales. A blue whale can eat as many as four million krill in a day.

FOUND IN:
Southern oceans

SIZE:
Up to 2 in long

SCIENTIFIC NAME:
Euphausia superba

Giant isopod

A sea-living relative of the wood louse, the giant isopod lives on the seabed where it eats any food it can find. Antarctic isopods are much bigger than those elsewhere in the world.

Sea spider

This spiderlike creature has a small body and 10 or 12 pairs of long walking legs, tipped with sharp claws. Male sea spiders also have an extra pair of legs for carrying eggs. When the female lays eggs, the male fertilizes them and collects them on his special legs, where they stay until they hatch.

FOUND IN:
Southern oceans

SIZE:
Legspan up to 10 in

SCIENTIFIC NAME:
Decolopoda australis

Antarctic cod

FOUND IN:
Antarctic coastal waters

SIZE:
40 in long

SCIENTIFIC NAME:
Notothenia coniceps

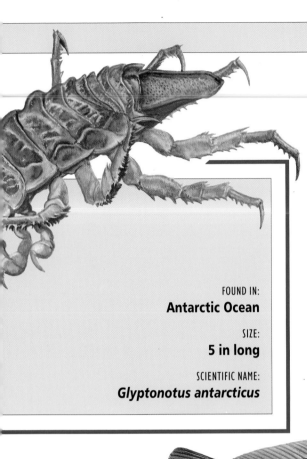

FOUND IN:
Antarctic Ocean

SIZE:
5 in long

SCIENTIFIC NAME:
Glyptonotus antarcticus

*I*cefish

The icefish is the only vertebrate animal that does not have the oxygen-carrying pigment called hemoglobin in its body. Without red blood cells, its blood appears almost clear and the internal organs are colorless.

FOUND IN:
Antarctic coastal waters

SIZE:
24 in long

SCIENTIFIC NAME:
Chaenocephalus aceratus

*A*rctic char

This cod spends much of its life on the seabed, where it feeds on worms, mollusks, and small crustaceans. It has a special adaptation for life in the Antarctic—its body contains an antifreeze substance which keeps the body fluids from freezing.

The Arctic char spends most of its life in polar seas, feeding on fish and mollusks. When ready to breed, it swims into Arctic rivers, where it lays its eggs among gravel on the river bed. The young eventually make their way back to the sea.

FOUND IN:
Arctic and North Atlantic oceans

SIZE:
Up to 38 in long

SCIENTIFIC NAME:
Salvelinus alpinus

Walrus

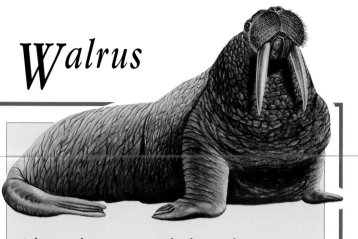

A huge, heavy animal, the walrus is covered with fatty blubber up to 4 inches thick, which keeps it warm in Arctic waters. Its tusks—actually teeth growing from the upper jaw—can be up to 3 feet long. The walrus eats mollusks and other bottom-living creatures and may use its tusks when searching the sea floor for food.

FOUND IN:
Arctic Ocean

SIZE:
Up to 11½ ft long

SCIENTIFIC NAME:
Odobenus rosmarus

Harp seal

The harp seal is an expert diver and a fast swimmer, using its hind flippers to push itself through the water. Most of the harp seal's life is spent at sea, but it does come to land to mate and to give birth to its young in early spring.

FOUND IN:
Arctic and North Atlantic oceans

SIZE:
Up to 6 ft long

SCIENTIFIC NAME:
Pagophilus groenlandicus

Leopard seal

Unusually slender, the leopard seal is built for speed. It is also a fierce hunter with a large mouth, well suited to catching penguins and even other seals. When it catches a penguin, the seal strips off the skin before eating it.

FOUND IN:
Southern oceans

SIZE:
Up to 11 ft long

SCIENTIFIC NAME:
Hydrurga leptonyx

White whale

The white whale is brownish when newborn, but it gradually becomes paler as it grows older. By the time it is six years old, it is a creamy-white color. White whales gather in huge herds of hundreds to migrate south in winter. They make a wide range of whistling sounds to keep in touch with each other—the reason for their old name, *sea canaries*.

FOUND IN:
Arctic Ocean

SIZE:
Up to 16 ft long

SCIENTIFIC NAME:
Delphinapterus leucas

Narwhal

FOUND IN:
Arctic Ocean

SIZE:
16 ft long

SCIENTIFIC NAME:
Monodon monoceros

The male narwhal has an extraordinary spiral tusk, made from an upper tooth. The tusk can grow up to 9 feet long. No one knows exactly why the male narwhal has this tusk, but it may be used as a weapon in battles with rivals for territory or mates.

Minke whale

Minke whales are common in the Antarctic. They filter plankton from the water through fringed horny plates of a material called baleen, which hang from the upper jaw. Whales that have these plates are called baleen whales; the minke is the smallest of these.

FOUND IN:
Polar and cool waters in all oceans

SIZE:
Up to 33 ft long

SCIENTIFIC NAME:
Balaenoptera acutorostrata

Focus on: Antarctic seals

There are no large land mammals in Antarctica, but plenty of seals thrive in the icy waters of the Antarctic Ocean. Seals are mammals that have become adapted to life in the sea. They spend much of their lives in the water, where they find their food, but they do haul out onto land or ice to rest or breed and to give birth. Seals are well suited to the cold. The body and flippers are covered with fur and they have a thick layer of fatty blubber under the skin that helps to keep them warm. Seals are expert swimmers and divers. When a seal dives, its blood flow is reduced to all but essential organs, such as the heart and brain, and its heart rate slows down. This means that the seal uses less oxygen than normal and can stay underwater for half an hour or more before having to surface and take a breath.

Ross seal
The smallest and rarest of Antarctic seals, the Ross seal measures up to 7½ feet long.

Basking elephant seals
Female elephant seals are almost half the size of males and do not have their characteristic large swollen nose. They give birth on land and feed their young for three to four weeks on their rich, nourishing milk.

Weddell seal
This seal is a deep diver, going down more than 2,000 feet and remaining under the water for more than an hour.

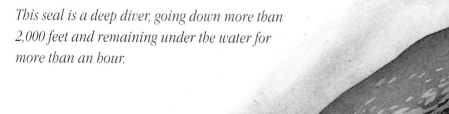

Crabeater seals

The most common seal, the crabeater is also one of the most abundant of all large, wild mammals. It feeds mainly on krill. It filters these small shrimplike creatures from the water, using its large interlocking teeth as a strainer. Crabeaters can move swiftly over ice, dragging themselves along with their front flippers at speeds of up to 15 miles an hour.

Elephant seals

A full-grown male elephant seal can be as much as 15 feet long and weigh up to 4 tons. In the breeding season, the males haul themselves out onto beaches and fight to win territory and females. Winning males gather a group of 20 or 30 females around them, which they defend from other males.

*E*mperor penguin

The largest of the penguins, the emperor breeds in huge colonies on the Antarctic ice. The female of a pair lays an egg in early winter. She then returns to the sea and leaves the male to incubate the egg on his feet beneath a warm fold of skin for about 60 days. He must not leave the egg for a moment and cannot feed. When it is time for the egg to hatch, the female returns and feeds the chick. The male is free to go and find food.

FOUND IN:
Antarctica

SIZE:
45 in tall

SCIENTIFIC NAME:
Aptenodytes forsteri

*W*ilson's petrel

This little seabird feeds mostly on small crustaceans. It plucks its food from the sea while hopping over the water's surface on its long legs. Wilson's petrel is thought to be one of the most numerous of all seabirds.

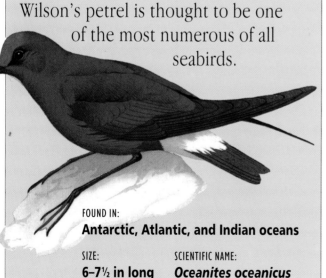

FOUND IN:
Antarctic, Atlantic, and Indian oceans

SIZE:
6–7½ in long

SCIENTIFIC NAME:
Oceanites oceanicus

*D*ovekie

FOUND IN:
Arctic and North Atlantic oceans

SIZE:
8–10 in long

SCIENTIFIC NAME:
Alle alle

Skua

A strong bird with a hooked beak and sharp claws, the skua gets much of its food by attacking other seabirds and stealing their catches. It also kills and eats smaller birds and their young.

FOUND IN:
Arctic and North Atlantic oceans

SIZE:
Up to 26 in long

SCIENTIFIC NAME:
Catharacta skua

Wandering albatross

FOUND IN:
Southern oceans

SIZE:
53 in long; wingspan: up to 11 ft

SCIENTIFIC NAME:
Diomedea exulans

This albatross has the longest wingspan of any bird. It spends most of its life soaring over the open ocean, flying as far as 300 miles in a day. It feeds on fish, squid, and food refuse from ships. It only comes to land to lay eggs and rear its young.

Vast numbers of these birds, also known as little auks, live in the Arctic. In the summer, they breed in colonies of millions on Arctic coasts and cliffs. Plankton and small crustaceans are the dovekie's main foods.

Ivory gull

The only all-white gull, this bird has a plump body and short legs. It is a scavenger and gets much of its food by following polar bears and feeding on the remains of their kills.

FOUND IN:
Arctic Ocean and islands

SIZE:
Up to 18 in long

SCIENTIFIC NAME:
Pagophila eburnea

Glossary

You may find it useful to know the meanings of these words when reading this book.

algae (*singular*, alga)
The simplest kinds of flowerless green plants, which grow in fresh water and in the sea. The smallest algae are tiny, each made of a single cell. Bigger algae form seaweeds.

anal fin
Fin on the belly of a fish near the tail.

blubber
The layer of fat under the skin of a marine mammal, such as a seal or whale. Blubber helps to keep the animal warm in the cold sea.

colony
A group of individuals of a single species living together in one place.

crustacean
A member of the invertebrate group *Crustacea*, which includes crabs, shrimps, and barnacles (see p. 11).

dorsal fin
Fin on the back of a fish.

gill
Parts of the body which water-living creatures, such as fish and invertebrates, use to take oxygen from the water. The oxygen passes into the blood.

gland
A part of the body that produces special substances, such as the fluids which harden into sticky threads to fasten a mussel to a rock.

invertebrates
An animal without a backbone. Invertebrates are often described as soft-bodied, but many, such as some kinds of crustaceans and mollusks, are covered with a hard protective case or shell.

larvae (*singular*, larva)
The young of an invertebrate animal such as a crab that looks very different from the adult.

mammal
A warm-blooded animal that gives birth to fully formed young. Mammals that have adapted to life in the sea include seals and whales.

mollusk
A member of the invertebrate group *Mollusca*, which includes clams, mussels, and octopuses (see p. 11).

mucus
Slimy protective substance covering the bodies of fish and some invertebrates, such as worms.

pectoral fins
The pair of fins on the sides of the body of a fish.

pelvic fins
The pair of fins on the underside of a fish. The pelvic fins are often below the pectoral fins, but the exact position varies in different species.

photosynthesis
The chemical reaction in which green plants trap energy from sunlight and use it to make foods, such as sugars, from water and the gas carbon dioxide.

plankton
Minute plants and animals that float in seawater. Many invertebrates and fish feed on plankton.

polyp
Individual sea anemone-like animals making up part of a coral colony.

predator
A creature that kills other animals for food.

prey
Creatures that are hunted and eaten by other animals.

reptile
A cold-blooded, scaly-skinned animal. Lizards, snakes, and turtles are all reptiles.

school
Group of fish or other marine creatures that swim together.

scavenger
A creature that feeds on the remains of animals that have died naturally or have been killed.

spawning
The process of producing large numbers of eggs by animals such as fish and frogs.

species
A particular type of animal. Members of the same species can mate and produce young that can have young themselves.

suckers
Disk-shaped sucking organ. The sucker of an animal such as a limpet attaches it to a surface. Suckers on the tentacles of animals such as the octopus are used to hold prey.

tentacle
A long, flexible structure, often around an animal's mouth, used for seizing food. Creatures such as sea anemones and octopuses have tentacles.

tide
Regular movements of the sea up and down the shore. In any one place there are usually two high tides and two low tides in any 24 hours.

vertebrate
Any animal with a backbone in its body. Fish, birds, reptiles, and mammals are all vertebrates.

Index

Acknowledgments

ILLUSTRATION CREDITS
Graham Allen: 24 (manatee, sea lion), 38–39 (blue whale, Dall's porpoise), 72–73 (white whale, minke whale)
Robin Boutell/Wildlife Art: 16–17, 36–37, 44–45, 62–63
Steve Kirk: 8–11, 14–15, 18–19, 34–35, 48–49, 56–57, 66–67, 70–71 (invertebrates)
Alan Male/Linden Artists: 24–25 (iguana, sea otter), 38–39 (dolphin, humpback whale), 72–73 (walrus, seals, narwhal)
Colin Newman /Bernard Thornton Artists: 22–23, 28–29, 30–31, 42–43, 46–47, 52–53, 60–61, 64–65, 70–71 (fish)
David Quinn: 25 (gull), 77 (skua)
Michael Woods: 20–21, 25 (Caspian tern), 32–33, 38–39 (frigate bird, tropic bird), 54–55, 74–75, 76–77 (except skua)

PHOTOGRAPHIC CREDITS
2 Kathie Atkinson/Oxford Scientific Films; 10 Peter Parks/Oxford Scientific Films; 12–13 Anne Wertheim/Oxford Scientific Films;
17 Anne Wertheim/Oxford Scientific Films; 21 Lon E. Lauber/Oxford Scientific Films; 26–27 Francois Gohier/Ardea; 33 David B. Fleetham/Oxford Scientifc Films;
36 Javed A. Jafferji/Oxford Scientific Films; 40–41 Lawrence Gould/Oxford Scientific Films; 44 Fred Bavendam/Oxford Scientific Films;
50–51 Peter Parks/Oxford Scientific Films; 54 Francois Gohier/Ardea; 58–59 David B. Fleetham/Oxford Scientific Films;
63 Pam and Willy Kemp/Oxford Scientific Films; 68–69 Tui de Roy/Oxford Scientific Films; 74 Doug Allan/Oxford Scientific Films